Jerome Donovan covers an important topic which has so far received little attention in the scholarly literature on the causes of war, namely the dynamics which led to the escalation of a regional conflict between Iran and Iraq to a full-scale war in the 1980s. He provides an integrated approach to the conflict and explains it in terms of the issues under contention, foreign policy reciprocity and power capabilities. Donovan points research toward the broader concerns of war causation as related to the issues that initially generate conflict between two states, the contextual features of the dyadic relationship which lead a conflict to evolve into a war, and the permissive and constraining features which allow for such an evolution. This book is a timely reminder of a war that continues to shape the politics of the region, as well as a significant contribution to international relations and conflict studies literature.

Amr G.E. Sabet,
Helsinki University

# The Iran–Iraq War

In a tradition that dates back to the time of Thucydides, and the Peloponnesian War, the systematic examination of conflict and war has long been a preoccupation of political scientists seeking to resolve the enduring question: Why do wars occur? This study directly engages this question with a specific focus on explaining the conflict between Iran and Iraq, arguably the longest and one of the more costly conventional wars of the twentieth century.

Explaining the systemic nature of conflict within the Middle East, and specifically between Iran and Iraq, the book illustrates how International Relations (IR) theory can be utilized in explaining conflict dynamics in the Middle East. The author's integrated approach to understanding interstate conflict escalation demonstrates that when taken together issues, interaction and power capabilities lend themselves to a much richer account of the dyadic relationship between Iran and Iraq in the lead up to war in 1980.

Addressing a disparity between International Relations and Middle Eastern area studies, this book fills an important gap in the existing scholarly literature on the causes of war. As such, it will be of great interest to scholars of peace and conflict studies, Middle Eastern studies and International Relations.

**Jerome Donovan** lectures in international studies at Swinburne University of Technology, Australia, before which he worked in the Royal Australian Air Force. Jerome has presented at international conferences and seminars in International Relations, International Studies, International Business and Political Science.

# Routledge Studies in Middle Eastern Politics

1 **Algeria in Transition**
  Reforms and development prospects
  *Ahmed Aghrout with Redha M. Bougherira*

2 **Palestinian Refugee Repatriation**
  Global perspectives
  *Edited by Michael Dumper*

3 **The International Politics of the Persian Gulf**
  A cultural genealogy
  *Arshin Adib-Moghaddam*

4 **Israeli Politics and the First Palestinian Intifada**
  Political opportunities, framing processes and contentious politics
  *Eitan Y. Alimi*

5 **Democratization in Morocco**
  The political elite and struggles for power in the post-independence state
  *Lise Storm*

6 **Secular and Islamic Politics in Turkey**
  The making of the justice and development party
  *Ümit Cizre*

7 **The United States and Iran**
  Sanctions, wars and the policy of dual containment
  *Sasan Fayazmanesh*

8 **Civil Society in Algeria**
  The political functions of associational life
  *Andrea Liverani*

9 **Jordanian-Israeli Relations**
The peacebuilding experience
*Mutayyam al O'ran*

10 **Kemalism in Turkish Politics**
The Republican People's Party, secularism and nationalism
*Sinan Ciddi*

11 **Islamism, Democracy and Liberalism in Turkey**
The case of the AKP
*William Hale and Ergun Özbudun*

12 **Politics and Violence in Israel/Palestine**
Democracy versus military rule
*Lev Luis Grinberg*

13 **Intra-Jewish Conflict in Israel**
White Jews, black Jews
*Sami Shalom Chetrit*

14 **Holy Places in the Israeli-Palestinian Conflict**
Confrontation and co-existence
*Edited by Marshall J. Breger, Yitzhak Reiter and Leonard Hammer*

15 **Plurality and Citizenship in Israel**
Moving beyond the Jewish/Palestinian civil divide
*Edited by Dan Avnon and Yotam Benziman*

16 **Ethnic Politics in Israel**
The margins and the Ashkenasi Center
*As'ad Ghanem*

17 **Islamists and Secularists in Egypt**
Opposition, conflict and cooperation
*Dina Shehata*

18 **Political Succession in the Arab World**
Constitutions, family loyalties and Islam
*Anthony Billingsley*

19 **Turkey's Entente with Israel and Azerbaijan**
State identity and security in the Middle East and Caucasus
*Alexander Murinson*

20 **Europe and Tunisia**
Democratization via association
*Brieg Powel and Larbi Sadiki*

21 **Turkish Politics and the Rise of the AKP**
Dilemmas of institutionalization and leadership strategy
*Arda Can Kumbaracibasi*

22 **Civil Society and Democratization in the Arab World**
The dynamics of activism
*Francesco Cavatorta and Vincent Durac*

23 **Politics in Morocco**
Executive monarchy and enlightened authoritarianism
*Anouar Boukhars*

24 **The Second Palestinian Intifada**
Civil resistance
*Julie M. Norman*

25 **Democracy in Turkey**
The impact of EU political conditionality
*Ali Resul Usul*

26 **Nationalism and Politics in Turkey**
Political Islam, Kemalism and the Turkish issue
*Edited by Marlies Casier and Joost Jongerden*

27 **Democracy in the Arab World**
Explaining the deficit
*Edited by Samir Makdisi and Ibrahim Elbadawi*

28 **Public Management in Israel**
Development, structure, functions and reforms
*Itzhak Galnoor*

29 **Israeli Nationalism**
Social conflicts and the politics of knowledge
*Uri Ram*

30 **NATO and the Middle East**
The geopolitical context post-9/11
*Mohammed Moustafa Orfy*

31 **The Kurds and US Foreign Policy**
International relations in the Middle East since 1945
*Marianna Charountaki*

32 **The Iran–Iraq War**
Antecedents and conflict escalation
*Jerome Donovan*

# The Iran–Iraq War
Antecedents and
conflict escalation

Jerome Donovan

Routledge
Taylor & Francis Group
LONDON AND NEW YORK

First published 2011
by Routledge
2 Park Square, Milton Park, Abingdon, Oxon OX14 4RN

Simultaneously published in the USA and Canada
by Routledge
270 Madison Ave, New York, NY 10016

*Routledge is an imprint of the Taylor & Francis Group, an informa business*

© 2011 Jerome Donovan

The right of Jerome Donovan to be identified as author of this work has been asserted by him in accordance with sections 77 and 78 of the Copyright, Designs and Patents Act 1988.

Typeset in Times New Roman
by Pindar NZ, Auckland, New Zealand
Printed and bound in Great Britain
by The MPG Books Group

All rights reserved. No part of this book may be reprinted or reproduced or utilised in any form or by any electronic, mechanical, or other means, now known or hereafter invented, including photocopying and recording, or in any information storage or retrieval system, without permission in writing from the publishers.

*British Library Cataloguing in Publication Data*
A catalogue record for this book is available from the British Library

*Library of Congress Cataloging in Publication Data*
Donovan, Jerome.
 The Iran–Iraq War: antecedents and conflict escalation / Jerome Donovan.
   p.cm—(Routledge studies in Middle eastern Politics)
   Includes bibliographical references and index.
   1. Iran–Iraq War, 1980–1988. 2. Iran–Iraq War, 1980–1988—Causes 3. Escalation (Military science) 4. Middle East—Politics and government. I. Title.
   DS318.85.D66 2011
   955.05'42—dc22                                          2010022664

ISBN 978-0-415-57989-6 (hbk)
ISBN 978-0-203-83935-5 (ebk)

# Contents

*List of figures* xi
*List of abbreviations* xii
*Acknowledgements* xiii

1 An integrated approach to understanding interstate conflict escalation: introduction — 1

2 An integrated approach to understanding interstate conflict escalation: theoretical foundations — 9

3 The pre-Algiers period: phase 1 of Iran–Iraq relations — 44

4 The détente period: phase 2 of Iran–Iraq relations — 68

5 The post-revolution period: phase 3 of Iran–Iraq relations — 86

6 Conclusions: explaining the Iran–Iraq war — 103

*Appendix 1* 111
*Appendix 2* 114
*Appendix 3* 116
*Notes* 118
*Bibliography* 129
*Index* 148

# Figures

| | | |
|---|---|---|
| 3.1 | Pre-Algiers total population | 57 |
| 3.2 | Pre-Algiers urban population | 58 |
| 3.3 | Pre-Algiers GDP | 59 |
| 3.4 | Pre-Algiers GDP per capita | 59 |
| 3.5 | Pre-Algiers military expenditure | 60 |
| 3.6 | Pre-Algiers military personnel | 61 |
| 4.1 | Détente total population | 74 |
| 4.2 | Détente urban population | 74 |
| 4.3 | Détente GDP | 75 |
| 4.4 | Détente GDP | 76 |
| 4.5 | Détente military expenditure | 76 |
| 4.6 | Détente military personnel | 77 |
| 5.1 | Post-revolution total population | 91 |
| 5.2 | Post-revolution urban population | 92 |
| 5.3 | Post-revolution GDP | 93 |
| 5.4 | Post-revolution GDP per capita | 93 |
| 5.5 | Post-revolution military expenditure | 94 |
| 5.6 | Post-revolution military personnel | 94 |

# Abbreviations

| | |
|---|---|
| Algiers Agreement | AA |
| Baathist Regime | BR |
| Balance of Power | BOP |
| Correlates of War | COW |
| Détente period | DP |
| Foreign Policy Reciprocity | FPR |
| Gross Domestic Product | GDP |
| Iran–Iraq War | IIW |
| Iraqi Communist Party | ICP |
| Persian Gulf | PG |
| Post-revolution period | PRP |
| Post-World War II | post-WW II |
| Power Transition Theory | PTT |
| Pre-Algiers period | PAP |
| Union of Soviet Socialist Republics | USSR |
| World Development Indicators | WDI |

# Acknowledgements

The study of conflict and war traces its history back to the time of Thucydides and the Peloponnesian War, with students and scholars alike engaged in the perennial search for an answer to the question of why wars happen. This study draws upon the empirical patterns and findings established in the works of many leading scholars including A.F.K Organski, Robert Axelrod, Kalevi J. Holsti, and Paul F. Diehl—to name but a few. In doing so, I would like to begin by expressing my deep thanks to them and acknowledge their work and the debt that is owed for their selfless contribution to our shared knowledge. It is from this foundation that I propose one method for reconciling the many instruments we now have for explaining conflict escalation and war.

Institutional support throughout this project has not been in short supply. First, I would like to express my thanks for the generosity and support provided to me during my time at the University of Tasmania, where I began this journey as a doctoral student. In particular, I would like to note the support and guidance of Matthew Sussex, who was pivotal in stimulating my interest in research on war causation. My sincere thanks also go to the research librarians at the Library of Congress in the United States of America who freely gave their time in helping this student find his feet during his research in their beautiful library.

More recently, my colleagues and faculty at Swinburne University of Technology have been instrumental in motivating me to complete this task. I would also like to thank Joe Whiting and Suzanne Richardson from Routledge for all their support and guidance throughout the process of getting this study ready for publication. Their input and interest have been invaluable in helping me reach this stage.

Perhaps most importantly, I would like to acknowledge the profound generosity and support that has been provided to me from all my friends and family. The network of people around me have enabled the long hours, missed weekends and holidays, and pressure filled moments to reach this pinnacle. In particular, I would like to give special thanks and acknowledgement to my parents, who have continued to be by my side throughout this entire experience. Words truly cannot express my appreciation to both my mother and father who have been unfailing in their endless support, understanding, patience, and encouragement. For this I am truly thankful.

# 1 An integrated approach to understanding interstate conflict escalation

## Introduction

In a tradition that dates back to the time of Thucydides, and the Peloponnesian War, the systematic examination of conflict and war has long been a preoccupation of political scientists seeking to resolve the enduring question: why do wars occur? This study directly engages with this question with a specific focus on explaining why the conflict between Iran and Iraq escalated to war in 1980. This conflict led to arguably the longest and one of the more costly conventional wars of the twentieth century. This conflict is interesting for a variety of reasons, not least because it has received relatively little attention in the scholarly literature on the causes of war. Most importantly, however, it represents a puzzle for some of the leading methods in analyzing the causes of conflict, in that concentrating exclusively on material capabilities, or alternatively emphasizing issues and foreign policy interaction, does not adequately explain the primary triggers for this war. Taken together, however, these methods allow for a more thorough understanding of why this war happened when it did.

Today, the occurrence of interstate war remains a rare event yet the extraordinary destructiveness, and enormity of stakes at play positions it as a central theme in international relations studies presenting students and scholars alike with an ongoing puzzle with the utmost importance to solve. The evolution of a distinct discipline studying international relations in 1919 at the University of Wales, Aberystwyth, saw a renewed focus on the systematic analysis of what causes interstate conflict. More recently, the contemporary student of war has faced a series of trends that appear to increase the complexities involved in explaining why wars happen. These include such factors as globalization, a surge in ethnic nationalism, and the spread of transnational terrorism. All of these seem to be driving states, groups, and even individuals towards the use of political violence to articulate their struggles or demands. While we are undeniably faced with an increasingly complex international environment, there is nonetheless a wealth of choice when selecting an appropriate instrument for the analysis of political violence. We have witnessed, for instance, the ongoing development of intensive research programs, such as the Correlates of War Project, Conflict and Peace Data Bank and World Event/Interaction Survey which provide increasingly rigorous ways for both measuring and understanding war. Yet in the post-Cold War world, where we have seen a proliferation of new methods purporting to explain the dynamics of conflict, the answer to the question of why war happens remains elusive. Michael Colaresi and William Thompson (2005: 346) recently discussed this abundance of choice, lamenting that "we lack many integrative theories linking [the] multiple causes of war escalation." This research represents an attempt to bridge some of these conceptual gaps. It is necessary to do so because it is unreasonable to progress to the analysis of 'new' or fourth generation wars,[1] if we are still unable to resolve existing problems in explaining interstate war, as the most familiar form of conflict experienced in the modern international system.

Traditional approaches have often concentrated on material capabilities or national power as the key determinants in understanding the actions of states. If one were to look at the most recent war between the "coalition of the willing" and Iraq in 2003, the association between access to energy resources and key US national interests has been widely identified as a major driver behind US policy.[2] In the post-invasion period, many analysts have continued to concentrate on the notion of national power and its distribution within geographic arenas. In particular, some have expressed the concern that the US invasion may have dramatically shifted the regional balance of power towards Iran, potentially destabilizing the Middle East.[3]

It is clear, however, that power alone is an inadequate basis from which to comprehensively understand the foreign policy behavior of states. A host of other complementary factors might also be useful in understanding conflictual or cooperative foreign policy behavior of states, and augmenting this traditional focus on the role of power.[4] Two additional methods are of particular interest in this study—interstate interaction and issues under contention. We narrow the focus to include these two additional methods in explaining conflict escalation due to their ability to identify patterns in the evolution of interactions between states (interstate interaction) and distinguish what states are fighting over (issues under contention). This will offer a historical context to the explanation of Iranian and Iraqi foreign policy interaction throughout the 1970s, illustrating how these states conflictual (and cooperative) foreign policy interaction led to war. At the same time, it will also allow the identification of the underlying reasons behind why these states were fighting.

Looking more closely, Axelrod and Keohane (1985) argue that the nature of interaction between states has a decisive impact on how relations evolve to the point of war. This may be explained mostly simplistically by the idea that war is considered to evolve from a "form of interaction between two or more states" (Geller and Singer, 1998: 22). Theorists take this further, however, arguing that relations between states are characterized by a high degree of reciprocity, particularly in self-help systems (Leng, 1993; Ward, 1982), with policy makers being driven by the type of behavior they receive from others. Behavior can become locked into a "tit for tat" scenario, whereby states continue to escalate the conflictual interaction (in the form of conflict cycles) by reciprocating and increasing the degenerative cycle between themselves. Issues are also thought to play an important role in the understanding of conflict and war, with the issues under contention between states forming the basis from which the disagreement and conflict evolves (Hensel et al., 2008). Issues are, in essence, what states are choosing to fight over and therefore provide important context in both what is stimulating war, and also directing policy makers towards the underlying problem to be addressed in preventing further conflict (Diehl, 1992).

Recent studies by leading researchers investigating both interstate interaction and issues-based explanations of conflict escalation are not in short supply. Examples include Rasler and Thompson (2006), and Hensel et al. (2008), who both study the relationship between issues and conflict escalation. On the interaction front, Crescenzi et al. (2008) and Leng (2004) have both further examined the role of international interactivity in foreign policy behavior. It is clear that these methods for understanding conflict escalation and war offer viable options for the examination of the Iran–Iraq War.

## 4  An integrated approach: introduction

Having said this, however, material factors still remain important in understanding the causes of war. A variety of methods are used in assessing the role of power in war causation, ranging from static assessments common to both balance of power[5] and power preponderance[6] arguments, to the dynamic approach offered by power transition[7] and power cycle theory.[8] Power can also be assessed at the systemic level through such approaches as polarity[9] or hegemonic stability,[10] each of which posit that the distribution of power within dyads, or regional and international systems, represent key elements in determining the behavior of states and thereby predicting the likelihood of conflict.

It is clear that issues, interstate interaction, and power offer researchers a variety of methods for explaining the causes of war. In fact, these three areas have formed cardinal themes permeating scholarly debate on the causes of the Iran–Iraq War. Here, one need only look to the most recent example of a study into this particular war's cause by Andrew Parasiliti in 2003. Parasiliti viewed the rising power of Iraq (and concomitant decline of Iran) as the key premise behind Saddam Hussein's decision to invade. Gholam Hossein Razi (1988), on the other hand, has argued that decision making elites in each country were more significant in deciding their future actions, with Ayatollah Khomeini's Pan-Shi'ism policy threatening Saddam Hussein's political legitimacy based upon secular and Arab nationalism—suggesting the importance of ideological issues in the evolution of their conflict to war. Efraim Karsh (1987/88) meanwhile has made an initial attempt to integrate the analysis of issues, interaction and power, looking at the interrelationship between foreign policy goals, their interaction, and military power in Saddam Hussein's decision to invade Iran.

Still others, like Will Swearingen (1988), Martha Wenger, and Dick Anderson (1987) have found that geography and resources were among the most salient issues stimulating this conflict. In fact, Swearingen argued for the reinterpretation of core ideological and demographic issues, such as the threat posed by the Shi'a majority in the south of Iraq and the Kurdish minority in the north, as being primarily within the realm of geopolitics, drawing analysis of the border dispute back some five centuries when Iran and Iraq were elements of the Persian and Ottoman empires. He claimed the reason for the war could be found in intrinsic disputes over territory.

Yet notwithstanding these studies' initial attempts to explain the causes of the Iran–Iraq War, it has not been as comprehensively analyzed as other more prominent conflicts within the region. Scholarly attention has been much more focused on inter-Arab politics and the Arab–Israeli conflict. This is understandable given that in the post–World War II period the Middle East has witnessed four major wars and numerous smaller conflicts as a result of tension between the Arabs and Israelis (Goldstein *et al.*, 2001). In fact, the existence of the Israeli state, along with the maintenance of its territorial sovereignty, continues to dominate academic interest within the region.[11]

It is a shame, however, that the Iran–Iraq War remains underexplored, because the scant existing explanations of this war's causes continue to be plagued by a number of problems. These include the lack of a systematic basis to explain the war and an overly narrow focus that overlooks the importance of relative power, foreign policy interactions and issues. For example, in Parasitili's (2003) analysis, the role of inter-Arab politics as a salient issue in stimulating conflict conflates the significance of external forces within a clear escalatory conflict cycle that had characterized Iran and Iraq's dyadic relations in the post-revolution period. Moreover, this analysis fails to account for important power conversion factors in the broad data used to assess the comparative power of Middle Eastern states. Similarly, while Razi's (1988) work in scrutinizing the foreign policy behavior of Saddam Hussein and Ayatollah Khomeini facilitates a deeper understanding of the dynamics of their behavior, it nonetheless fails to account for why the war happened when it did, with no systematic calculation of the role of capabilities in allowing Iran and Iraq to fulfill their foreign policy goals and issue resolution.

Whilst Karsh (1987/88) offers perhaps the most comprehensive and integrative approach to the study of the Iran–Iraq War, it too is not without fault. His exploratory study reviews the interaction between Iran and Iraq, as well as focusing on issues under contention and military power capabilities. In doing so, Karsh articulates the importance of interaction between Iran and Iraq throughout the period leading to the war, the host of issues that were evident in their relationship, and illuminates the evolution of their comparative military power capabilities. He does not, however, identify which of these issues are most salient, nor does he address their interaction in a comprehensive manner. Moreover, he only examines the effect of military expansion in the comparative power capabilities of Iran and Iraq during the period, without capturing other important bases of national capabilities which impacted upon their relationship.

Finally, Swearingen's (1988) focus on the importance of geo-political issues, and in particular the predominance of territory in stimulating this conflict, does not account for the importance of hard power capabilities in constraining the escalation of hostilities between Iran and Iraq. This was particularly the case in 1975, where relations between the two had neared the point of war, with similar underlying territorial issues that were present when the war began in earnest in 1980. Yet paradoxically, 1975 heralded the Algiers Agreement between the two nations, which ushered in a period of détente.

Consequently, we not only face a range of approaches that may be applied in the explanation of wars' causes, but also a case that warrants further examination. The key question I turn to now is whether an explanation based on the three leading approaches identified here— issues, interaction or power analysis—can best explain the causes of this conflict. This question informs the rest of this study, and I develop an answer over the course of subsequent chapters.

In Chapter 2, I investigate the utility of issues, interstate interaction and power-based approaches to the analysis of wars' causes, arguing for an integrative approach in studying interstate conflict escalation. I begin by examining issues-based explanations for conflict escalation and war causation, illuminating the importance of highly salient issues in explaining what states are fighting about. In doing so, I identify a method for categorizing the issues under contention, and determining the level of salience of these issues for the states involved. Next, I move on to critically surveying the interstate interaction literature, and identify reciprocity as an effective method within this area for explaining how dyadic relations between states evolve to the point of war. Moreover, foreign policy output is identified as the key measurement focus, allowing for the delineation of patterns in interactions between states through a focus on actualized policy. As a result, it helps us understand how inter-state hostilities escalate to war.

I subsequently undertake an assessment of the static and dynamic basis for the explanation of power and war in dyadic relationships. I demonstrate that static approaches—balance of power and power

## An integrated approach: introduction 7

preponderance—can be utilized in the explanation of war causation, although they both fail to account for an important characteristic of power: change over time. I find that a dynamic basis of power analysis, through Organski and Kugler's power transition theory, provides a potential way forward in explaining changes that occur in dyadic power distribution, which can be used to identify conditions in which conflict and war are more likely. In concluding this chapter, I identify three distinct phases in the relations between Iran and Iraq preceding the onset of the war in 1980.

In the following three chapters I assess the utility of this integrated approach to understanding interstate conflict escalation on explaining the Iran–Iraq War, beginning with Pre-Algiers period. In Chapter 3, I demonstrate how the relations between Iran and Iraq evolved from the British announcement of its impending withdrawal from the region. This set the course for Iranian regional aspirations, with the Shah determined to project Iranian dominance over the Persian Gulf, and subsequently led to the abrogation of the London treaty of 1937 which had been regulating the border between Iran and Iraq. A reciprocal and escalatory conflict cycle evolved as these states contended over the underlying issues stimulating their interaction. Relations escalated to the precipice of war in 1975, where the analysis of power capabilities demonstrates the constraining force of Iranian power preponderance on the further escalation of the conflictual interaction.

In Chapter 4, Iranian and Iraqi relations are shown to evolve from the Algiers Agreement, which had seen the resolution of the underlying issues stimulating conflict in the Pre-Algiers period. Intermittent and cooperative moves where illustrated in their interstate interaction, occurring with the backdrop of evolving domestic instability in Iran with the revolution, and the rapid convergence in comparative power capabilities between the two countries. The period concluded with the installation of the revolutionary government in Iran, and the subsequent dramatic shift in policy preferences, and underlying issues of contention between the two states.

Chapter 5 concludes the examination of relations in the period preceding the onset of the Iran–Iraq War. The revolutionary Iranian government enacted a policy of Pan-Shi′ism, aimed at stimulating revolutionary change within the region. The articulation of the Iranian's desire for revolutionary change resulted in a direct threat to their neighbors, including

## 8  An integrated approach: introduction

Iraq, who sought to secure their security and maintain their independence from Iran. A conflictual and escalatory conflict cycle emerged as Iran and Iraq contended over these two issues, evolving to the point of war in September 1980. It is at this point where power transition theory is utilized to demonstrate the permissive conditions that existed, with Iraq having experienced a rapid convergence and transition in power capabilities. The Baathist party was no longer constrained in resolving their issues through the continued escalation of force, leading to the invasion of Iranian territory on the night of September 22, 1980.

The integrated approach to understanding interstate conflict escalation proves useful in further explaining why the Iran–Iraq War happened when it did. With the issues-based explanation illuminating the underlying reasons for these states fighting, foreign policy reciprocity demonstrating how their interactions evolved to the point of war, and power transition theory identifying the permissive conditions for continuing the escalation of conflict to war. In doing so, this approach provides a richer explanation for why the war between Iran and Iraq occurred when it did.

Chapter 6 concludes with a review of this study's three main conclusions on the utility of the integrated approach to understanding interstate conflict escalation in explaining the Iran–Iraq War. It highlights some of the key issues identified in the application of issues under contention, power transition and foreign policy reciprocity theory to empirical tests. I also illuminate potential avenues for future studies into war causation.

# 2 An integrated approach to understanding interstate conflict escalation
## Theoretical foundations

In this chapter I critically evaluate three mainstream methods for understanding the causes of war: issues, interstate interaction and power analysis. Within these fields are a variety of approaches that may be utilized in explaining their relationship with conflict escalation and war, yet three emerge as the leading instruments—issues under contention, interstate reciprocity (also referred to as foreign policy reciprocity), and power transition theory. While each of these instruments offer the ability to independently analyze why the Iran–Iraq War occurred, an integrated approach to understanding interstate conflict escalation is pursued here. This approach, I argue, demonstrates that when taken together issues, interaction, and power capabilities lend themselves to a much richer account of the dyadic relationship between Iran and Iraq, and offer a more thorough explanation of why the war happened when it did.

Although stopping short from advocating a formal synthesis of these instruments, the integrated approach to understanding interstate conflict escalation allows the illumination of the contextual developments in Iran and Iraq's interaction while appreciating changes in their material capabilities. More specifically, the examination of issues under contention allows this approach to distinguish the reasons why Iran and Iraq were fighting in the lead up to war in 1980. Foreign policy reciprocity identifies the distinct patterns of interaction in their foreign policy behavior when seeking to resolve the issues under contention, ultimately leading these states to the precipice of war. Finally, the examination of dynamic power capabilities allows this approach to chart the permissive and constraining material forces on the type of foreign policy behavior utilized in seeking the resolution of their highly salient issues, generating conditions in which Iran and Iraq were more likely to continue escalating their conflictual interaction to war.

This integrated approach to understanding interstate conflict escalation is not alone in seeking to utilize indicators from a variety of different theoretical schools. Indeed, Geller and Singer (1998: 6) argue for a broader variety of indicators to be utilized in testing historical records of conflict and war, and point to academic aspirations for more integrative approaches asserting the need for "considerable openmindedness toward conflicting explanatory models of world politics, coupled with a strong commitment to systematically examining the evidence in support of them." One needs only to look, for instance, at the recent work by Lahnerman (2003) and Doran (2003), where positivist approaches to the examination of power have been adapted to incorporate the analysis of foreign policy behavior. Doran (2003) sought to establish a relationship between power and foreign policy roles, looking at these two factors as coequal in explaining the international interactions of states. Lahnerman (2003) went beyond Doran's recognition of the dual role foreign policy and power play in the articulated or intended actions of states at the international level, and sought to evaluate their impact on stability or instability. In doing so they attempted to reconcile competing theories of state behavior while reinforcing the role of power in determining state behavior.[1]

Issues-based theorists have also been particularly active in utilizing more integrative approaches; one such example is in Hensel *et al.* (2008) whose study examines three territorial issues as sources of interstate conflict. In their study they also utilize three other methods in examining conflict outcomes including recent issue management, relative capabilities and the presence of a joint democracy. Another such example can be seen in the broad based study implemented by Prins (2005), who sought to capture the role of rivalry in conflict escalation utilizing the evolutionary model of interaction, controlling for the effect of regime type, power, and the characteristics of the crisis. Earlier examples can also be found of integrative approaches including in the work of Brewer (1973) whose study sought to capture previous involvement between states from an issues-based approach.

In addition to the mainstream scholarly efforts at pursuing a broader based approach to explaining conflict escalation and war, previous studies analyzing the Iran–Iraq War have also attempted to incorporate such

An integrated approach: theoretical foundations    11

an approach. Several examples have been highlighted, including the studies of Karsh (1987/88) and Parasiliti (2003), with both these authors making initial—albeit limited—efforts at incorporating an appreciation of the issues, interstate interaction, and comparative power capabilities in the lead up to the Iran–Iraq War in 1980. This study builds beyond these previous attempts, refining the theoretical basis from which to examine this war. I now turn to establishing the theoretical foundations for issues, interstate interaction and power analyses of war causation, illustrating empirical support for these methods. I subsequently review why the Iran–Iraq conflict has been chosen as the case study, and what is expected from this integrated approach to understanding interstate conflict escalation when examining this war. This chapter concludes with an overview of the three phases to be utilized in examining Iranian and Iraqi relations.

## Issues under contention

Looking first at issues, these are thought to play an important role in determining the behavior of states[2] and can be described simply as the "subjects of disagreements between nation-states" (Hensel et al., 2008: 118). Proponents of the issues-based approach believe that foreign policy interaction is directed by issue contention, by which states behavior is influenced by the type of issues involved.[3] Diehl (1992: 333) takes this one step further, suggesting that issues explain "what states choose to fight over, not the conditions that led to the choice of military force as the means." Issues should therefore not be deemed as "sufficient conditions for war" (Holsti, 1991: 17) in their own entirety; rather, they should be viewed as an underlying, rather than proximate, cause of conflict and war (Petersen, 2008; Vasquez, 1993; Vasquez and Henehan, 2001). The presence of contentious issues, in tandem with how they are handled by the actors involved, can increase or decrease the probability of states becoming involved in conflict and ultimately war. Indeed, as Diehl (1991: 333) argues, issues are "an important factor in the decisions to use military force and escalate the dispute to full scale war."

The inclusion of issues into the research agenda on exploring why some conflicts end in war stems from its ability to tell us "what men are likely to fight about" (Holsti, 1991: 12). Holsti (1991: 12) goes further arguing that "it is hard to see how this critical question, even if posed only in descriptive terms, can be ignored any longer." Despite this importance, the incorporation of issues into political analysis has been inconsistent (Diehl, 1992), and some would go so far as to argue 'deleterious' (Rosenau, 1967). McLaughlin-Mitchell and Prins (1999: 169) more recently reinforced this position, suggesting that scholars "have been slow to address the fundamental issues that ground interstate conflict." Empirical research has concentrated primarily on national, dyadic and systemic explanations of state behavior (Diehl, 1992; Holsti, 1991) at the expense of a consideration of the issues under dispute (McLaughlin-Mitchell Prins, 1999; Luard, 1987). Holsti (1991: 14) believes the shift from this traditional approach focusing on the antecedent conditions to an issues-based approach would create a teleological explanation with "wars occur[ing] not 'because of' but 'in order to'."

Research has periodically responded with the adoption of an issues-based paradigm to explaining the evolution of conflict to war, yet as noted above, empirical research has been slow in maintaining pace with the calls for further research (Mansbach and Vasquez, 1981; Diehl, 1992; Hensel, 2001). Some argue[4] that problems have resided in the difficulty with defining and measuring issues, while others such as Hensel (2001: 81), suggest one of the key inhibiting factors in the empirical examination of issues is "the lack of issues data in existing social science data sets and the difficulty of collecting original data related to issues." Despite these difficulties in incorporating issues into the research agenda on conflict and cooperation, Holsti (1991: 12) contends that "to leave out issues is to leave out the stuff of politics."

This study recognizes the importance of understanding the issues under contention and the value they have in providing a basis for understanding what states are fighting about. As a result this study builds on the approach put forward by Hensel (2001), Diehl (1992), Rosenau (1966), Brewer (1973) and Vasquez (1983)—among others—in concentrating on the role of issues in the evolution of conflict and war, and more specifically on issue salience.

*Issues and foreign policy behavior*

Many theorists have sought to capture the role of issues in influencing foreign policy behavior of states. One such example is by Zimmerman

(1973), who offered a basic interpretation of how issue areas can stimulate foreign policy behavior, and consequently result in conflictual interactions leading to war. He develops an argument based on a continuum of issues at stake, with states viewing issues from either a pole of power or of indifference. If the issue at stake is within the pole of power, it is much more likely to be related to a significant value held by a state—such as its preservation or territorial integrity—and therefore more likely to result in power maximizing behavior (i.e. the use of force). Conversely, if the matter is not important, and classified within the realm of indifference, it is unlikely to result in the utilization of power maximizing behavior by the state. Zimmerman's (1973) argument offers a basis from which to understand the importance of issues, their corresponding values to the state and the likely impact on conflictual foreign policy behavior.

More recently Hensel (2001) clarified the conceptual basis for the incorporation of issues into the study of conflict arguing that these studies are grounded in three central and underlying themes which differentiate them from more traditional approaches to the explanation of conflict and war. That is, foreign policy is directed by issues, issue characteristics make a difference to foreign policy behavior, and both conflict and cooperation are substitutable foreign policy tools that can be utilized by states in addressing issues.

Looking more closely, issues-based theorists argue for the centrality of issues within foreign policy interactions, characterizing the interchange between the actors involved (Mansbach and Vasquez, 1981; Diehl, 1992; Luard, 1987; Rosenau, 1967; Vasquez, 1993). Hensel (2001: 81) takes this one step further, arguing that states do not simply react to structural considerations such as polarity or comparative national power positions, but rather they pursue a directed series of decisions "in order to achieve their goals on a variety of different issues." In doing so, it is thought that policy decision makers are concentrating on attaining value satisfaction, where issues are simply representing certain key values held (Mansbach and Vasquez, 1981). These values often have abstract and intangible attributes (such as security, status, or freedom), and therefore are pursued through specific stakes with which policy makers can attach more "concrete and tangible objects" (Hensel, 2001: 81). Values and stakes are often linked to form a specific issue area over which states can thereby contend over.

14  *An integrated approach: theoretical foundations*

When states decide to pursue a particular type of foreign policy behavior—be it conflictual or cooperative—it may have stemmed from one of many issues that have evolved over a long period of time (Bercovitch and Jackson, 1997). Most foreign policy interactions take place over an extended period, allowing the actors involved to reframe and adjust the issues under contention, resulting in the view that "multiple interlocking issues are seen to be at stake" and the struggle between the actors becomes increasingly laden with symbolic meaning (Bercovitch and Jackson, 1997: 14). This leads to the second central theme, emanating from the multiplicity of issues that may be embedded in any ongoing conflict or cooperation between states. That is, the importance of issue characteristics in influencing the type of foreign policy behavior pursued by the actors involved (Hensel, 2001).

As at any point in time there may be a multiplicity of issues on the policy agenda, the issues under contention only impact upon the foreign policy of states through the level of salience that is attached by those involved (Luard, 1987). That is to say, the more that the actors value a particular issue under contention, and the impact of its resolution, the more likely it is that this will generate greater involvement by the associated actors, and thereby potentially creating more chances of conflict or cooperation. Hensel (2001: 83) also notes that much of the empirical research into issue salience and foreign policy behavior has been centered around conflict, with little "known about nonmilitarized attempts to manage or settle issues."

Building beyond this, it is also thought that issue salience will direct the amount of resources that states are willing to expend in achieving that goal (Hensel, 2001). Low salience issues will be unlikely to create a situation where states pursue risky military action, as the decision to implement military options does not guarantee a positive resolution. Likewise, this argument can be extended to highly salient issues. When states view the failure to achieve a particular goal as more costly, they are more likely to also utilize force despite the costs and risks associated with doing so.

This argument builds on earlier work of leading researchers including Rosenau (1966), Brewer (1973) and Vasquez (1983) who classify the salience of issues on the degree of tangibility they are characterized by Rosenau (1966) classified issues into four groups including status (which have intangible means and ends), territorial (intangible means and tangible ends), human resource (tangible means but intangible ends), and non-human resources (and tangible means and ends) issues. Rosenau (1966) determined the expected type of foreign policy behavior depended on the tangibility of the means and ends. Brewer (1973) further specifies Rosenau's (1966) typology contending that ends relates to values allocated and means relates to the resources utilized in achieving the ends.

Rosenau (1966) believes the more intangible the ends the more likely it is to stimulate ongoing contention between participants, and consequently, conflict. The key to Rosenau's analysis is that the issue attributes will stimulate conflictual or cooperative interaction between states. As intangible ends are often associated with highly ideological issues, and are often difficult to disaggregate, it is more likely therefore to result in the difficulty to compromise producing a winner-takes-all scenario. In doing so, states have the option of either pursing the intangible goal further, for which conflict will become more likely, or alternatively abandon it. The choice of the two options is dependent on the overall salience of the issue to policy makers, linking back to the importance of issue salience in determining a state's willingness to pursue a particular issue on their agenda.

It should also be noted that the salience attached to different issues is subject to variation depending not only on the actor, but also on the temporal period or region in which it occurs (Luard, 1987). Luard (1987: 131) highlights this fact, arguing that it is not clear whether or not some issues are more likely to bring about war than others, but it is clear that "questions that seem of vital national importance in one age, and a justifiable cause of war, in another are matters of indifference." Luard (1987) separates the examination of issues into distinct periods of time including the age of dynasties (1400–1559), religions (1559–1648), sovereignty (1648–1789), nationalism (1789–1917), and the age of ideology (1917 onwards).

Holsti (1991: 280) concurs with this argument suggesting that issues generating conflict change over time, and that we currently "live in an age of economic resources, nationalism, religion, ideology, state creation, national security, ethnic affiliation, territory, spheres of influence (regional domination), and many other values coexist and frequently conflict." Moreover, he suggests that the post-WW II era has seen the emergence of two different systems from which issues evolve, with the mature system characterized by consolidated boundaries and well-integrated societies. This is in contradiction to the other system, which is new, does not have a well established system of boundaries and governance, and is characterized by many internal threats. The players in the new system are concerned with the maintenance of state sovereignty, developing national identity, controlling their populations and establishing stable borders (Holsti, 1991). The issues that these states find salient are fundamentally different.

The third central theme of issues-based research is that states have the ability to pursue the attainment of issues through the utilization of either cooperative or conflictual policy tools (Hensel, 2001). Luard (1987: 128) argues that war is simply one "instrument which can be utilized in pursuit of many quite different aims, if it is seen, in particular circumstances, as the best means available for promoting that cause." Although the ability of states to draw on both conflictual and cooperative foreign policy tools has been recognized theoretically, this has received limited empirical attention within the research on issues (Hensel, 2001). More recently, Hensel et al. (2008) have described a broader scope of both cooperative and conflictual policy tools that states can draw upon in resolving issues under contention. They argue that states might choose to negotiate bilaterally, or through third parties. Actors also might choose non-binding or binding agreements or even a range of foreign policy behavior short of war including threats of force or displays of capabilities (Hensel et al., 2008).

Actors, therefore, have the ability to call on a wide selection of "alternative mechanisms for allocating the disputed stakes" (Hensel, 2001: 83). Conflict and the use of force are more likely, however, when the states seeking to resolve their issues are confronted by incompatible values and interests from the other party involved (Holsti, 1991: 24). Luard (1987: 129) extends the link between issues and war, suggesting that war is mostly likely to occur when states believe they have a "legitimate claim to particular kinds of trading right . . . or to control of a particular waterway . . . or to a piece of territory." Issues-based theorists have also identified that the history of how the issue has been dealt previously being an important consideration in predicting future efforts—and methods—to resolving the issue (Brewer, 1973; Hensel et al., 2008; McLaughlin-Mitchell and Prins, 1999; Vasquez, 1983).

## An integrated approach: theoretical foundations 17

One of the earlier empirical examinations undertaken into the relationship between issues and foreign policy behavior was by Brewer (1973), who explored four common typologies of issues and their ability to identify discernable patterns in foreign policy behavior. His findings demonstrated that issues do indeed provide a basis from which to explain some variances in how policy elites respond to different foreign policy problems. He also found that interaction over these issues was a critical factor in determining the behavior of these states, with attempts at isolating events or cases obscuring a clearer picture of why the states are fighting over the issue under contention.

Another early study undertaken by Vasquez (1983) built specifically on the issue typology developed by Rosenau, testing the tangibility of issues and foreign policy behavior. He found that, in general, foreign policy behavior will become more cooperative as issues become more tangible. Likewise, more conflictual behavior is associated with increasingly intangible issues. This conflictual behavior was further attenuated by the presence of more actors being involved, one resource being employed, behavior is persistent with regard to the issue, other issues are not involved, increased frequency of interaction over the issue, and either diplomatic or economic resources being utilized.

Empirical support was also provided for the role of different issues in stimulating conflict when Mansbach and Vasquez (1981) examined the relationship between stakes under contention (without clustering into issue areas) and the event interactions of US and West German actors. During the period 1949–75, they found the control of stakes under contention allowed for a clear delineation over what caused conflictual behavior. For example, they found that the conflictual interaction between the Soviet Union and the US spiked at 85.7 percent of interactions when dealing with West German security, compared with no conflict when dealing with the commitment of Western allies to Berlin. They argue that "the failure to control for stakes may blur the sources of conflict within dyads" (Mansbach and Vasquez, 1981: 873).

More recently studies examining the role of issues in foreign policy behavior and interstate interaction have sought to extend their analysis to include other pertinent variables. Gibler (1997), for example, examined issues-based conflicts, extending the analysis to include the effects of alliances on the settlement of disputes. He finds alliance commitments can contribute towards the management of conflict, and

## 18  An integrated approach: theoretical foundations

in particular, when removing territorial issues as a point of contention. McLaughlin-Mitchell and Prins (1999) also expanded the examination of issues and militarized conflict to include the examination of differences in regime type. In their examination of democratic disputants, they found that territorial issues were much more likely to experience reciprocal conflict cycles, with these disputes being reciprocated more than twice that of non-territorial disputes (90 percent and 39.5 percent, respectively).

Petersen's (2008) study has also extended significantly the parameters of issues-based explanations of conflict, undertaking a comprehensive examination into the effect of regime type, capabilities, alliances, and contiguity on conflict escalation. She found that territorial issues were very contentious, irrespective of regime type, although it was in liberal democracies where a particularly high rate of militarized interstate disputes escalated to war (with one in ten, compared with one in fifty for illiberal democracies).

One of the foremost experts in the issues-based paradigm to understanding foreign policy behavior, Paul Hensel, has also been particularly active in propelling a broader research agenda, with the inclusion of other variables including past interaction and power capabilities (Hensel, 1999; 2001; Hensel and McLaughlin-Mitchell, 2005). In a collaborative project in 2008, Hensel *et al.*, (2008) built on previous studies which had relied on the identification of issue type, positing that the recent interaction, salience, and type of issues are important determinants in revealing when states are more likely to resort to conflictual management techniques. They found that the utilization of both conflictual and cooperative methods of issue resolution is more common when the salience of the issue is higher, and that recent issue interaction "increase[s] pressure to take further action to settle the issue" (117).

They also utilized two control variables, regime type and power capabilities, showing that conflict is less likely when it is between a dyad which is not evenly matched in capabilities, or are democracies. Looking more closely at power capabilities, although a static measure was utilized (derived from the Correlated of War project, based on the composite index of national capabilities), this finding provides further support for the importance of drawing in the permissive or constraining national attributes that influence a states likelihood of utilizing war as a

## An integrated approach: theoretical foundations 19

method for resolving issues under contention. It is an important extension to the study of issues, which this current study intends to develop further utilizing dynamic measures of power capabilities.

Issues have therefore been shown to provide a useful basis in understanding what states fight about, with salience driving certain issues to the forefront of competition between states, and conflict or cooperation both being possibilities of the competition that takes place in resolving the issues under dispute. It is now important to determine how issues will be captured in this study.

### Classifying issues

This study builds upon both a broader typology of issues and an abstract categorization of issue salience in determining the role of issues in the relationship between Iran and Iraq. This study will then be both descriptive and explanatory, allowing the generalization of the findings at the same time maintaining the cohesiveness and descriptiveness of the unfolding processes (and issues under contention) between Iran and Iraq. Often, Holsti (1991: 17) argues, "there is not always a very good fit between the typologies of academics and the issues as they were defined by the actors involved in conflict."

This study will utilize Holsti's (1991) typology of issues as the basis in identifying the issues under contention during the periods under analysis. It will also utilize Hensel, Mitchell, Sowers and Thyne's (2008) issue salience categorization in determining the overall salience of the issues under contention. In doing so, this study can capture what the issues are, how these issues change over time, how they evolve to the point of war, and how multiple issues are incorporated into the policy agenda between the warring parties.[5]

### Issue typology

Holsti (1991) develops a comprehensive typology of the different conflicts that have characterized the post–World War II period, which provides a useful basis in identifying what types of issues are under contention. According to Hensel et al., (2008: 119), the list developed by Holsti "has provided the most comprehensive categorization by listing dozens of issues that have been at stake in war since 1648."

Although this has only been intended to provide a descriptive list of possible issues, we utilize his post–World War II issue categories as the starting point in identifying the different broad categories of issues that are evident, distinguishing the issues under contention between Iran and Iraq. He identifies that there are seven key types of issues that formed the basis of contention during this period within the international system—territory, nation-state creation, ideology, economics, human sympathy, predation and survival, and other issues.

Looking first at territory, Holsti (1991: 307) contends that territory as a basis for war revolves around the "control, access to, and/or ownership of physical space." Although this issue has seen a gradual decline in prominence as a source of conflict and war, it still continues to influence policy decisions, particularly through a geo-strategic rationale. That is, states continue to position the control over particular territory offering avenues for attack or important commerce routes, as central to their security problems. Nevertheless, territorial expansion has been largely removed as a contentious issue, with the rationale that control over significant territorial expanses may in fact create a weakness for states, due to the need to maintain administration over it and the higher probability that different religious or ethnic groups may inhabit that territory (which may in turn seek secession).

Despite its decline from prominence, many researchers have recognized territory as being highly correlated with conflictual interactions. Bercovitch and Jackson (1997: 13), for example, suggest that "territory and sovereignty are by far the most potent factors" in war causation. This, they argue, is derived from the key foundation of all states being derived from their sovereignty over a particular land area. Territory as an issue has been highly conceptualized, as it is viewed as amongst the "most salient of all possible issues" (Hensel, 2001: 85). It is important, however, to recognize that territory is "only one issue and not even the most prevalent in the post-World War II time period" (McLaughlin and Prins, 1999: 169).

Nation state creation issues are the second categorization of issues identified.[6] This forms a broader aggregate of national liberation, unification/consolidation, and succession issues, and accounts for some 52 percent of the issues under contention in the post–World War II era. Holsti (1991) aggregates these issues into the broader category as they have similarities across values, stakes and behaviors, and share the underlying purpose of achieving statehood. More recently the drive towards statehood, according to Holsti (1991), has stemmed from a group's ethnic/religious/language commonality and desire to be identified through a legitimate political entity.

According to Holsti (1991: 311) "men have frequently gone to war over ideas," and increasingly the international political arena has been characterized by disputes over ideas. This issue can be captured through looking at the ideological aspirations and political principles of the parties to the conflict, and can be both from governments afar and near.[7] Ideological issues may be from the perspective of a foreign power concentrating on the control or influence of other governments, or the desire to replace or undermine the political ideology of foreign regimes. This issue most commonly takes form in the "attempts to influence and control political change abroad" (Holsti, 1991: 311).

Economic issues revolve around the desire of states to establish preferential or exclusive market and resource access, protect property and investments of citizens in foreign states, or even to ruin the trade of rival powers (Holsti, 1991). This was a particularly prolific issue in past wars, particularly when buttressed by mercantilist theories of a state's power position. It has, however, declined as an issue in war during the post–World War II period.

Sympathy, be it for religious, ethnic, or ideological kin, can also be an issue for which states choose to fight. According to Holsti (1991) the sympathy factor has played an important role throughout the periods examined in his study, with states inclined to utilize armed force in preventing the physical harm, persecution, or even threat of harm, from being directed upon their kin. This also includes not only the outright protection of kin in other countries, but can also result in irredentist claims over neighboring territory. Sympathy can be more difficult as well to appease, should two states be contending over it as an issue.

Survival emerges as an issue from conflicts where states seek to "eliminate another state or regime as an officially independent political entity," while predation refers to "the attempt to destroy a regime or dismember, partition, or liquidate a sovereign state" (Holsti, 1991: 318). Often this is also referred to as total war, seeking the removal of the opposing state. Although this has declined as an issue in the post–World War II period, it nevertheless remains above 21 percent of all conflicts and is viewed as an important issue in the escalation of conflict to war (Hensel *et al.*, 2008; Holsti, 1991).

And the final major category of issues in the post–World War II period is what Holsti (1991) refers to as 'other issues'. In this group he amalgamates together a range of other less prevalent—although reoccurring—issues that are linked with warfare, including state/imperial integrity,[8] and regional dominance. State or imperial integrity can stem from challenges of national liberation by ethnic and religious minorities. Regional dominance is aimed at maintaining control or pre-eminence in the determination of regional policy and state behavior.

*Issue salience*

Building from Holsti's issue typology, issue salience relates to the degree of importance that people or their leaders place on the issue at stake (Diehl, 1992; Hensel *et al.*, 2008; and Randle, 1987). Diehl (1992: 341) argues that "salience is one of the characteristics of issues that likely influences the chances for war." In measuring issue salience, the relative salience of a particular issue under contention should not be assumed to be asymmetric between the parties involved (Diehl, 1992); rather, it should be noted that for one party it may have very little consequences, while for the other it might be of fundamental significance. Any approach, therefore, that seeks to capture the salience of the issues involved should utilize a composite measure that captures the salience of the issue for both parties involved. Moreover, issues are not always the same for both parties involved but rather states may contend over similar stakes derived from other issues of importance.

We utilize the more recent conceptualization of issue salience developed by Hensel *et al.* (2008) who focus on the intangible and tangible values associated with the issue under contention. This method allows for capturing issue salience from both parties, overcoming the issue identified by Diehl (1992) regarding the asymmetric assumption in issue salience. Hensel *et al.* (2008) lay the foundation for their work from values identified in the studies of Lasswell and Kaplan (1950), Maslow (1970), and Mansbach and Vasquez (1981), and argue that the following values are critical in understanding international cooperative and conflictual behavior:

Intangible Values
- Equality/Justice: values focused on the equal, fair and impartial distribution of resources, etc.
- Culture/Identity: values associated with an identity, religion, culture or ideological beliefs.
- Status/Prestige/Influence: values linked with how one is treated by others, including the level of respect afforded.
- Independence: freedom associated with developing and following independent policies.

Tangible Values
- Survival: ability to fulfill basic human needs including food, water and shelter.
- Wealth: extending from the basic necessities, this focuses on the accumulation of more money, goods or resources.
- Security: absence of external danger, including threats.

The utilization of value tangibility remains consistent with the issue typology identified by Holsti. This delineation of values underlying the issues under contention is a simple extension from issue identification, allowing the determination of issue tangibility through the associated values. Hensel, Mitchell, Sowers, and Thyne (2008) do not attempt to rank the overall priority of each of these values, preferring to remain agnostic over their relative worth for each state as the comparative importance of these values is bound to be different depending on the position and priorities of each individual and group. They do, however, rank the issues associated with these values on salience. In doing so, their work develops from that of Vasquez (1983), Rosenau (1966 in Farrell, 1966), Brewer (1973) and others who have focused the coding of issue salience along the lines of tangibility and intangibility.

Issue salience levels are determined by categorizing the issue along the two dimensions of tangibility or intangibility, being either of high or low values. According to Hensel, Mitchell, Sowers, and Thyne (2008), to achieve a 'relatively high' value status the issue should be of importance to either the leadership or the majority of the population for the states involved. Likewise, to be classified in the 'relatively low' category, the issue should not have any significant salience for the Parties involved. A variety of issues can be classified as having high salience values on either tangible or intangible dimensions, although for those issues classified as having high overall salience the two most common tend to related to territory and regime change (Hensel et al., 2008).

Issues that tend to have low salience on both the dimensions of tangibility are often associated with a narrower sub-set of the population, such as individuals or organizations. Hensel, Mitchell, Sowers, and Thyne (2008) draw on examples of trade disputes arising from unfair governmental treatment of domestic industries and anti-competitive actions against foreign organizations, and also foreign government treatment of individuals within their borders. While there is some intangible and tangible value associated with these different issues they are unlikely to resonate with the broader population or state leadership.

Based on their classification of tangibility dimensions from either high or low salience levels Hensel, Mitchell, Sowers, and Thyne (2008) develop broad groupings of issues. High salience issues are those that rate highly on both intangible and tangible dimensions, medium salience issues rate highly on one dimension (but not both), and low salience issues obviously score low on both dimensions.

The issues-based approach therefore offers a method for understanding what states are fighting about, with the identification of the most salient issues between warring parties. Although this is useful in identifying what states are fighting about, it does not however elucidate the process of how states arrived at the point where they were willing to fight over these issues, nor the conditions that permit them to do so. The concept of interstate interaction offers valuable insights into understanding the process by which states' relations evolve over time and develop to the point of war.

**Interstate interaction**

While the issues under contention may set the scene for what states are fighting about, it is the context in which an issue takes place which is often argued to have the most "decisive impact on its politics and its outcomes" (Axelrod and Keohane, 1985: 227). Issues evolve through a prism of past interactions and future expectations of states, coloring how these issues will be dealt with (Axelrod and Keohane, 1985;

An integrated approach: theoretical foundations 25

Hensel, 2001). The foreign policy tool that is therefore utilized—be it conflictual or cooperative—in attempting to achieve an outcome to the issues under contention develops in parallel with the interstate relations of the parties involved.

Looking more closely at interstate relations, it is recognized that relations develop over time, creating "mosaics of past interactions" (Crescenzi and Enterline, 2001) from which political leadership can be informed of their counterpart's likely behavior in given situations. Moreover, the interactions between states are characterized by a "high degree of reactivity" (Ward, 1982: 87), where the behavior that a state receives is likely to be returned in like (Axelrod, 1990; Leeds and Davis, 1999). Leng (1993: 3) takes this argument one step further, suggesting that the reciprocation of behavior between states functions as the principle norm of interaction in self-help systems. Goldstein and Pevehouse (1997: 515) also support this view, arguing that a strategy of reciprocity is particularly well suited in an "'anarchic' realm of international relations, where states operate autonomously in pursuit of self-interest."

This idea of reciprocity guiding interstate behavior evolved from a research agenda beginning in the 1960s, when the Richardsonian 'stimulus-response' approach was initially established (Goldmann, 1980; Richardson, 1960). His approach to modeling arms races was further pursued in the later work of Wallace (1979) and Diehl (1992), and has since extended to a broad range of studies including on game theory and reciprocity by Axelrod (1990) and dynamic interstate cooperation and conflict with the likes of Rajimaira and Ward (1992), Goldstein (1995) and Kinsella (1995). More recently the study of interstate interaction and reciprocity has been extended to rivalries, such as in the work of Goertz and Diehl (1995), and issues-based explanations of conflict with Hensel (1996; 1999).

These studies have all built upon the central concept of strategic interaction and reciprocity between states in the international system. Despite earlier claims by Goldstein and Pevehouse (1997) that this critical concept suffers from a persistent "dearth of systematic empirical work on reciprocity," it has been demonstrated above that a large number of studies have begun to clarify and refine the utilization of this theory. This research now turns to the further conceptual development of reciprocity and interstate interaction, building on the seminal work of Robert Axelrod (1990), and the more recent work of Mark Crescenzi and Andrew Enterline (2001).

## Reciprocity and interstate interaction

As mentioned above, interstate reciprocity studies have evolved from the 'stimulus-response' approach put forward by Richardson in 1960. Stated simply, interstate reciprocity holds that the behavior a state experiences within a particular relationship strongly influences its own behavior.[9] Reciprocity[10] offers researchers a method for identifying distinct patterns of behavior within dyadic relationship between states.[11] It assumes that actions or policies of states within a dyad will mutually evolve. By extension, if states within a dyad are involved in hostile diplomacy, reciprocity suggests that war will be the likely outcome.

One of the foremost theorists in establishing the reciprocal link between basic interactions of states has been Robert Axelrod, who in his pioneering work *The Evolution of Cooperation*, developed a basic framework upon which to analyze interactive behavior in dyadic relationships. Axelrod (1990: 3) posited the central question: will cooperation develop in an anarchic world, and under which conditions? His answer was a theory of cooperation from the Iterated Prisoner's Dilemma game, in which there are two actors. These two states, or "players," have two primary choices in their interactions (namely, to cooperate or defect). During their interaction, these states can choose either of two possibilities. If one chooses defection it can gain the greatest return, if the other state continues to cooperate. At the same time, if both states within this dyadic relationship defect, then both will be worse off than if they had both cooperated (Axelrod, 1990).

Axelrod drew on a pertinent example at the time in which he was writing: the Soviet invasion of Afghanistan in 1979. The invasion presented the US with a dilemma whereby if it were to continue with "'business as usual' the Soviet Union might [have been] encouraged to try other forms of non-cooperative behavior later on" (Axelrod, 1990: 7–8). Conversely, if action were taken by the US to respond, lessening its degree of bilateral cooperation in an era of détente, Soviet retaliation might have resulted, with subsequent escalations resulting in a potential conflict spiral.

## An integrated approach: theoretical foundations  27

Axelrod's model of interaction is concerned more with an indefinite number of interactions, as opposed to single or sporadic interaction.[12] This reflects the idea that cooperation becomes more rational for states within a dyadic relationship if the immediate payoffs of a defection are placed within the "shadow of the future":[13] that is, immediate benefits garnered by defection will pale in comparison to the potential for future benefits to be gained through cooperation.

Axelrod (1990: 20) thus proposed that a simple strategy of "tit for tat," in which a state cooperates on their first move and "then does whatever the other state did on the previous move", emerges as a successful method for an analysis of interaction. The successful fulfillment of "tit for tat" is subject to the existence of four key properties, identified by Axelrod (1990: 20) as (i) reciprocating the cooperation by the other state, thereby avoiding unnecessary conflict; (ii) responding likewise to the defection by the opposing party; (iii) potential for forgiveness following a response to the defection; and (iv) clear and consistent behavior enabling the other state to adapt its own patterns of action.

A final important element exists within the theory of reciprocity, in terms of the nature of change that is experienced in reciprocal bilateral relations within a dyad. According to Axelrod, the simple "tit for tat" characterizes reciprocity in cooperative relationships. Obviously bilateral relations between states cannot be limited to cooperation, as conflict does indeed occur. Axelrod (1990) does highlight that not all relationships exist within a cooperative framework, and that those that experience conflict cycles may experience dampened echoing effects. That is, actors may decide to return only nine-tenths of a "tit for tat," allowing for a de-escalation of dyadic conflict.

A more recent attempt at characterizing change in reciprocal relations has been made by Mark Crescenzi and Andrew Enterline (2001). Crescenzi and Enterline contended that relationships can either move, or experience growth, towards solidifying a particular type of behavior (whether cooperative or conflictual), just as in nature. And, as the behavior can experience growth, so too can it experience decay (Crescenzi and Enterline, 2001). Representing a dynamic model of interstate interaction, they argued that the degree to which this change affects the interaction between states is determined by two factors. These are the degree to which change is experienced, and the temporal distance since the previous event occurred (Crescenzi and Enterline, 2001).[14]

Arguably, as this study seeks to explore the relationship between the study of policy and the escalation of interstate interactions to war, the model for change attributed to Crescenzi and Enterline has many benefits, particularly the acknowledgement that the interactions between states can be, and often are, characterized by conflict. Moreover, it is instructive that these interactions can indeed experience a process of escalation, the outcome of which can be war, as opposed to cooperation.

The claim that bilateral dyadic relationships tend to be reciprocal has also been supported by a study undertaken by Joshua Goldstein, Jon Pevehouse, Deborah Gerner, and Shibley Telhami (2001). They showed that "in nearly all dyads characterized by serious conflict, reciprocity was significant" (Goldstein et al., 2001: 593). Their work also revealed that bilateral reciprocity occurred within dyads despite the relative nature of power distribution (balanced or imbalanced) between states. Their empirical findings provided limited support for the idea that bilateral reciprocity can lead to the emergence of cooperation in the Middle East (Goldstein et al., 2001). The India–Pakistan dyad is another example that has received the attention of reciprocity theorists, especially when the relationship was marked by chronic animosity and conflict between 1950 and 1992 (Rajimaira, 1997).

Brett Ashley Leeds and David R. Davis (1999) also found evidence of reciprocity in the interaction of states within dyads. Many of the cases they examined indicated that states do indeed tend to respond reciprocally to the actions of other states, with reciprocity forming the norm of dyadic interactions irrespective of whether the relationship was characterized by conflict or cooperation.

Reciprocity also holds firm beyond dyadic interactions, with Joshua S. Goldstein and Jon C. Pevehouse (1997) demonstrating that regional conflicts are also characterized by reciprocity. The example they drew upon was the Bosnian conflict from 1992 to 1995, which involved NATO, Serb, and Bosnian forces. Goldstein and Pevehouse found that reciprocity characterized the conflict interaction between NATO and Serb forces, particularly following the Serbian military strikes against the Bosnian government.

Another example of foreign policy reciprocity in action was demonstrated by Michael Ward (1982), who examined the relationship of policy interaction between states focusing on two broad models: a behavior-begets-behavior; and mix-of-behaviors-begets-mix-of-behaviors. His analysis showed that the first model (behavior-begets-behavior) was substantially more common than a mixed model (Ward, 1982: 94). Now that we have the method for which to capture the interstate interaction between Iran and Iraq, the question emerges on what basis do we measure this? The answer to this question is through employing foreign policy output analysis.

## Measuring interstate reciprocity through foreign policy output

Looking more closely at foreign policy analysis, this involves examining the fundamental processes and actions taken by distinct actors (or groups of actors), in attempting to define or redefine their societal dynamics, derivative of an innate sense of practical reason towards a given end: in this case, a war to achieve a given outcome.[15] Foreign policy behavior can be broadly categorized into three main types of analysis—input,[16] process,[17] and output.

In this study we focus on foreign policy output analysis as it is based upon, first and foremost, tangible policy. This consists of the international and domestic aims and objectives sought by a state, expressed at either the international or national level. Policy can be simply articulated, or visible through a particular action.[18] As soon as policy has been produced, either through a proclamation or an act, it sets up an interactive process of fulfillment that places a demand on the environment. Until the point where active attempts are being made to fulfill the policy desires of the government, policy is solely within the realm of the "state's 'internal affairs', ambitions, dreams, ideals" (Levi, 1970: 3).

This follows the approach utilized in many reciprocity studies including Rajmaira and Ward (1990), and Colaresi and Thompson (2002), in which the focus is on output analysis—or the outcomes—where actualized behavior places demands on the environment in which this policy will be fulfilled. This also fits with the nature of interstate interaction we seek to examine; necessitating state's to actualize their policy intent to influence the behavior of other states.

An example of articulated policy can be seen in a statement released by the Shah of Iran in 1969, stating that "when the British leave, Iran can do it [expand into the Persian Gulf], because we have no territorial

## 30  An integrated approach: theoretical foundations

or colonial designs" (cited in Friendly, 1969: 15). He was referring to the impending British withdrawal from the region, and was setting the ground work for expanding the Iranian sphere of influence. Iraq, on the other hand, elicited its policy of confrontation against Iranian expansion through its actions, mobilizing and deploying its troops to their mutual border and ejecting Iranian citizens residing in Iraqi territory (Durdin, 1969: 2; *Los Angeles Times*, 1969: 15).

Foreign policy reciprocity (FPR) therefore offers a method to show how relations between states evolve through delineating patterns of behavior, where states conform to a 'tit for tat' scenario, including in the escalation of conflict to war. We now have a basis for understanding what states are fighting about, and a process from which to understand the escalation of conflictual interaction to the point of war. However, what we do not yet understand is the permissive or inhibitive forces that influence these states in deciding to escalate their conflictual interaction over a particular issue to war. It seems obvious that the willingness of states to allow the continuation of conflictual relations to war in the pursuit of issue resolution must be done so through a lens of capacity.

## Power analysis

Power theorists agree, and seek to explain the interactions between states through comparing each state's capabilities. Power acts as both an enabling and constraining force in the articulation of a state's desires, and can influence another state into acting in a way it would not have done otherwise.[19] A wide variety of methods can be employed in determining the role of power in war causation, ranging from the more static measurements seen in the balance of power argument[20] and power preponderance,[21] to the dynamic analysis seen in power transition,[22] or the systemic based perspectives of polarity and hegemonic stability theory.[23]

As this study is focusing on the dyadic analysis of Iran and Iraq, it is therefore possible to narrow this selection to the two principal units of dyadic measurement: static and dynamic measurements of power (Geller, 1993). These two methods of assessment form the principal approaches applied by theorists[24] seeking to explain the dyadic relationship between power and war. Within the static field of study the role of power is generally perceived as impacting upon the onset of war in two opposing ways—balance, and preponderance, of power (Siverson and

Sullivan, 1983). Within the dynamic field of study, power is generally considered with reference to the power transition theory proposed by Organski and Kugler (1980).

## Static power analysis

Balance-of-power (BOP) theory is perhaps the commonest means to understand power. Balance-of-power theorists claim that the international arena and the distribution of resources within this arena is a zero-sum game (Horowitz, 2001). A comparatively equal distribution of power among states, in particular major powers, is meant to encourage stability (Siverson and Sullivan, 1983). Competition for the distribution of resources can nevertheless result in shared gains, and jockeying for position between states (and groups of states) can result in a "balanced" system (Garnham, 1976).

A central argument of balance of power theorists is that equality in the distribution of both power and resources contributes to establishing and maintaining peace, as no side will be dissatisfied with the system (Claude, 1962; Geller, 1993: Niou and Ordeshook, 1986; Waltz, 1979). The existence of two states, or groups of states relatively equal in their power capabilities will result in neither being certain of victory, and as a result both will be deterred from war.[25]

A recent study by Matthew Rendall (2006), demonstrates the continuing utility of balancing arguments, with a positive correlation between the pacific outcome of four situations and the balanced power argument. A further example of support for balancing arguments can be found in Bruce Bueno de Mesquita's (1981) work. Using a composite capabilities index he found that between 1816 and 1965 some 75 percent of victors in wars were stronger than their opponents prior to war.

In direct opposition to balance of power arguments are power preponderance studies. This concept directly contradicts balance of power theory, arguing that a disparate relationship in power between states will result in the stronger nation not needing to employ force, as the weaker state will not be capable of resisting its demands (Siverson and Sullivan, 1983). Its proponents, like Stuart Bremer (1992), have argued that power preponderance promotes peace, since a weaker side would clearly avoid being drawn into war, when the likely outcome would be to lose.[26]

Power preponderance theory supports the view that when nations are near parity in terms of capabilities, each will believe it has a probable chance of winning. As such, this encourages preemptive action (Siverson and Sullivan, 1983). This holds that the existence of a BOP situation in fact increases the incidence of war, as decision makers believe they are better placed to succeed when preponderance does not exist on the other side (Organski, 1968 cited in Garnham, 1976).

For instance, William Moul (2003) examined the relationship between major powers in the years between 1816 and 1989, and found support for the supposition that a relative parity between power capabilities encouraged war. Likewise, a study undertaken by Daniel Geller (1993: 173) on the impact of power differentials on war within rival dyads found, through the analysis of 456 militarized disputes occurring between 1816 and 1986, that power parity and shifts toward parity are "approximately twice as likely to be associated with war as ... power preponderance." This gives rise to some initial validation for the argument that preponderance encourages peace.

### *Static power analysis: a conundrum?*

While both balance of power and power preponderance approaches put forth strong theoretical arguments, they also offer divergent and contradictory empirical evidence. Daniel S. Geller (1993: 176) recognizes this point, suggesting that:

> A considerable amount of research has [already] been conducted regarding the effects of different dyadic power distributions on the frequency, magnitude, and severity of interstate conflict and war; and unfortunately the findings on static balances are inconclusive.

This is not to say that power does not play a role in war causation, or even that the difficulties encountered by these approaches in accurately measuring its influence means that we should discount their importance. Rather, as Randall Schweller (1997: 927) noted, it is clear that history shows both preponderant and balanced systems have existed, and do explain the interaction of states. However, a fundamental error underpinning this contradictory evidence is the assumption that power is static and that it should be measured thus (DiCicco and Levy, 1999).

In fact, changes regularly occur in both the relative and comparative power capabilities of states over time, and require a more dynamic measurement to account for this change. Fortunately there is a basis for undertaking such an investigation: power transition theory (DiCicco and Levy, 1999).

## Dynamic power analysis

### Power transition theory: a way forward

In order to overcome the problem of static power and consequently enrich our understanding of its role, recent research has increasingly measured power as a dynamic variable in the onset of war.[27] Power transition theory, like power preponderance, proposes that conflict is more likely to occur when a dyad is characterized by rough parity.[28] Yet it also takes its analysis of power further (Geller, 1993). Power transition theorists hold that the analysis of power and war should be from the perspective of both static variables, such as preponderance, and a dynamic variable to determine the real impact of power in the occurrence of war.

Power transition theory thus recognizes that balance of power and power preponderance theories still have much to offer the analysis of power and war (Lemke, 1997). It is evident, however, that they are unable to establish a whole picture of the relative or comparative power capabilities that states possess. Both power preponderance and balance of power theories provide the framework with a method which achieves 'snapshots' of the comparative and relative relationship of participants.

Power transition theory, on the other hand, moves beyond this, arguing that there is a hierarchy of power (as opposed to the focus of many structural realists, such as Kenneth Waltz, on international anarchy) that influences the nature of international, regional, or even dyadic relationships. This is typically characterized by the emergence of one key state, or coalition of states, which seek to control the rules and values enforced within the system (Geller, 1993).[29] Competition ensues, with the power distribution subjected to flux and change with the emergence of new states within the international system.[30]

Power transition theorists believe that as a result of this competition, changes occurring in the comparative power position of states within a dyadic relationships can result in a power transition.[31] Underpinning this is the recognition that power is not a constantly stable, absolute variable, which will enable an analyst to view any snapshot in time, undertake a power analysis, and arrive at an explanation for the international outcome witnessed. Rather, the only constant that an analyst can be sure of when analyzing power is that it will change (Gochman and Moaz, 1984). As Douglas Lemke correctly notes, by utilizing a dynamic method of analysis power transition theory thus recognizes the inherently unstable and unpredictable nature of power, and its ability to change and fluctuate depending on the environment in which it is measured (Lemke, 1997).

Power transition theorists seek to measure these changes in the comparative power position of states, and associate three key conditions of change with the increased likelihood of war: comparative transformation, convergence, and transition.[32] Power transition thus overcomes the fundamental weakness of balance of power and power preponderance theory, which relies on a static basis of analysis. The importance of the dynamic nature of power is clearly evident when analyzing the period prior to the Iran–Iraq War. If one were to take a snapshot at the beginning of the 1970s, assessing Iran's national power, it would show that it was reaching a relative peak in its comparative superiority over Iraq. However, by 1979 the capabilities Iran possessed were seriously inhibited by domestic instability, creating a significant decline in power (particularly military capabilities).

Likewise, change is unmistakably evident when reviewing the relative power capabilities of Iraq. At the beginning of the period Iraq's overall power capabilities were undermined by social instability caused by the Kurdish separatist movement. However, by the end of the period, after a process of domestic consolidation, Iraq had experienced a dramatic increase in both its relative and comparative power position with that of Iran.

Indeed, if one were to look beyond the case at hand, the changing nature of dyadic power distribution forms a foundation upon which many studies are evaluating future Sino-American relations. These seek to assess the potential effect of change or transition in the comparative power relationship between the US and China through the use of power transition theory in an attempt to determine the likelihood of future conflict (Chan, 2005; Casetti, 2003; Rarkin and Thompson, 2003).

The first comprehensive statistical test of the relationship between power transition and war was undertaken by A.F.K Organski and Jacek Kugler in 1980. Their study utilized a dynamic method of analysis to assess the role of power in affecting the likelihood of war. Findings from their study provided some initial insights into the relationship between global leadership and power transition, showing that no wars have taken place without some form of power transition (be it a transition before, during, or after the war).

More recent research has continued to support this proposition. For example, Kim Woosang's (2002) study found a positive correlation between the role of power transition in war causation, by examining conflict in East Asia.[33] William Reed (2003) also provided some empirical support that power transition theory can pinpoint the onset of hostilities, demonstrating that as states converged on power parity, uncertainty increased the likelihood of militarized conflict.

A study undertaken by Jeffrey Morton and Harvey Starr (2001) also found support for war being more likely to occur when power fluctuations are evident, as opposed to static systems in which power is constant. In their study, Morton and Starr found that pre-fluctuation periods experienced fewer wars (at 21 percent) than fluctuation periods (with some 44 percent of the cases leading to war).

A particularly interesting example of support for the power transition theory can be found in the work of Douglas Lemke (1997), who suggests that this theory can be utilized to explain why the Cold War never evolved to war. He argues that as the Soviet Union (the weaker power) never achieved parity with the US, war was never likely between the two. Lemke demonstrates that the Soviet Union was barely able to achieve a comparative GDP half that of the US. As a result, Lemke suggests that this approach can both explain peace and war.

One final important example of empirical evidence supporting the relationship between power transition and war can be found in the work of Indra de Soysa, John Oneal, and Yong-Hee Park (1997). De Soysa et al. (1997) showed, using COW data, that out of 33 dyads identified as experiencing a power transition, 14 (42 percent) experienced war within a 20-year time frame. In these cases De Soysa et al. (1997: 520) noted that transitions occurred before war. This analysis showed that 33 percent (or 7 of 21) dyads with less than a 20 percent difference in power capabilities experienced war, while only 20 percent (or 13 of 65) dyads with power capability differentials of greater than 20 percent went to war. It is evident from this that strong support exists for the notion that war is more likely to occur when power transitions occur, especially when they are characterized by a reversal in comparative levels of power. Even GDP data showed that a transition was again the primary indicator of war with 43 percent (or 13 of 30) of transitory dyads experiencing war.

These studies reflect the need to take seriously the idea that changes that occur in the relative and comparative power capabilities have a dramatic effect on the likelihood of war. Having established that power capabilities play an important role in determining the behavior of states, and in particular creating a permissive or inhibitive force on articulating forceful behavior such as war, it is now important to establish how this study intends to capture national power.

## *Measuring dynamic power capabilities*

The measurement of national power presented here stems from two primary data sources—the Correlates of War Project and Economic Capabilities—most commonly utilized in the study of power transition theory. I also follow Joseph Nye's (1990) suggestion regarding the incorporation of power conversion factors when assessing the realized national power of these states, and utilize two additional country-specific factors to supplement this analysis, reflecting the importance of power conversion in actualized capabilities. Power conversion is about the ability to translate potential power in the form of resources into realized power. Often the measurement of power is based on the assumption that countries can convert material resources into capabilities with the same efficacy as others. However, as Joseph Nye (1990: 178) argues, it is clear that "some countries are better than others at converting their resources into effective influence." If one were to consider the example of World War II, as Nye (1990: 178) does, the fact that France and Britain had more tanks than Germany in 1940 did not prove to be an effective capability restraint, as Germany maintained greater maneuverability and strategy.

Nevertheless, looking first at the base indicators to be utilized in determining national power, from the COW Project and Economic Capabilities, three specific elements of national power are consistently demonstrated to be of great importance: military power, demographic indicators, and economic capability. Military power and demographic indicators form two[34] of the key elements utilized by the COW Project in determining national capabilities.[35] Economic capabilities are also routinely utilized to form an independent measure for the assessment of national power.

Demographic indicators are thought to provide a broad capability index of a states' overall power capabilities, and provide an additional source for the development (or hindrance) of a state's military capabilities. Demographic indicators can assist with an evaluation of a state's overall power capabilities through two primary indices: total population and urban population.[36] Total population is often utilized as a composite of state power as a large population (i) can be translated into a large army; (ii) can assist in maintenance of domestic industries during periods of conflict; and (iii) can enable a state to absorb losses incurred during hostilities (Singer et al., 1972). Urban population, meanwhile, can also give an indication of a state's power. This occurs through the utility of its "association with higher education standards and life expectancies, with industrialization and industrial capacity, and with the concentrated availability of citizens who may be mobilized during times of conflict" (Singer et al., 1972).

Military power capabilities are those capabilities that will be employed or utilized in the event of war, and will form the basis of a state's ability to enter into combat either for defence or offence. Military power capabilities are derivative of material resources that directly impact upon the composition, form, or type of military force a state possesses. Two of the most common indices in which military power capabilities are measured are through military expenditure and military personnel.[37] Military expenditure provides a basis for understanding the amount of resources available to the armed forces of a state, and can determine its capability to recruit, train, and maintain military personnel. Moreover, it can demonstrate the potential of an armed force to acquire, introduce, and maintain military equipment. The measurement of military personnel illustrates the number of troops under the command of a government that can be used to conduct military operations, be it for defence or offence (Singer et al., 1972).

Economic capabilities have the ability to portray both the size and rate of development or decline in a nation's economy,[38] and underpin other

## 38  An integrated approach: theoretical foundations

capabilities such as military power and demographic indicators.[39] Two key measurements are especially pertinent here—GDP and GDP Per Capita. GDP is used to measure the aggregate product of a state, and is thought to show a state's ability to not only support its military goals, but also its economic and political actions.[40] It can also demonstrate the amount of potential resources that a state may draw upon, should the need arise (Casetti, 2003). On the other hand, GDP Per Capita provides an indication of the development of an economy, indicating the quality of a state's GDP position relative to its total population (Casetti, 2003).

The final two indicators—military modernization and absorption, and social stability—are country-specific factors that influence the translation of economic, demographic, and military resources into realized power capabilities. Their incorporation into a broader based assessment of national power reflects the importance of power conversion in the translation of material resources (such as a large population and extensive military expenditure) into actualized power.[41] As Joseph Nye (1990: 17) argues:

> Some countries are better than others at converting their resources into effective influence . . . Thus one has to know about a country's skill at power conversion as well as its possession of power resources to predict outcomes correctly.

Here, military modernization and absorption relates to the translation of military expenditure into military power capabilities. Military expenditure is by nature focused on modernizing forces and allowing the introduction of modern military platforms, bringing both Iran and Iraq's armed forces into the era of more advanced warfare. It is therefore important to determine the efficacy of translating material resources attached to military expenditures into power capabilities. Social stability is linked to demography, and relates to issues that impact upon the translation of the population into a realized power. It incorporates the impact of social and ethnic mobilization on the ability of the state to utilize its population for productive use in domestic industries, or the armed forces.

The case of the Iran–Iraq conflict is particularly suited to the examination of issues under contention, foreign policy reciprocity and the

## The Iran–Iraq War: expectation from issues under contention, foreign policy reciprocity, and power transition theory

Beginning on the night of September 22, 1980, when Iraqi jets crossed into Iranian territory to launch a preemptive strike, the Iran–Iraq War was to become the longest conventional interstate war of the twentieth century. Lasting for some 95 months, it finally concluded in August 1988, when the Iranians accepted a UN-mandated cease-fire (Hiro, 1989; Gongora, 1997; Mofid, 1990; Renfrew, 1987).

The prolonged duration of the Iran–Iraq War distinguished itself from other third world wars, such as between India and Pakistan,[42] or the series of Arab–Israeli conflicts,[43] which had been characterized by brevity (with some of these conflicts limited to only several weeks or months). It was marked by a drawn-out series of bouts between these two countries, and its extended duration allowed both sides to continue supplementing their supplies of military equipment.

It pitted these two competing regional powers in a struggle with Iraq, on the one hand, looking to take up the mantle of regional Arab leadership, following the Camp David Accords and the subsequent demise of Egypt as a major power on the Arab front (Dawisha, 1980; Neff, 1991; Parasiliti, 2003). Iran, on the other hand, was arguably the most powerful Persian Gulf state throughout the beginning and middle of the 1970s, buttressing Western interests within the region against Soviet pressure (Mearsheimer and Walt, 2003).

Both Iran and Iraq experienced significant damage to their societal structure, economies, infrastructure, and service industries (Razi, 1988). Whole cities, such as Khorramshahr, Basra, and Abadan experienced substantial damage throughout the conflict (Razi, 1988). Some have attempted to quantify the degree of damage, with estimates of US$1.1 trillion dollars of destruction and over one million casualties.[44] The war absorbed domestic economic capabilities, with Iran and Iraq consuming some 60 percent and 112 percent of their GDP, respectively, to finance the ongoing conflict (Gongora, 1997). It was, in effect, a large, long, and classic example of interstate war for the

## 40  An integrated approach: theoretical foundations

twentieth century. Yet previous explanations of this conflict are discursive and disparate, with the causes of the conflict remaining elusive even today.

As noted earlier, one of the most recent examples of a study into the causes of this war has been by Parasiliti (2003) who, although highlighting the importance of material factors in enabling Iraq to invade Iran, failed to systematically examine the issues under contention and overlooked the cyclic nature of their interactions that had been characterized by a "tit for tat" scenario throughout the period. Similarly, Karsh (1987/88) illustrated the importance of issues, their interaction and military power in directing the actions of Iraq, yet failed to implement this in a systematic manner. Other prominent examples of studies into this conflict, such as by Razi (1988) or Swearingen (1988), utilize singular approaches purporting to the importance of either material or political factors in their explanations, and fall short from offering a comprehensive evaluation of the conflict.

So we have a case that warrants further examination due to its significance as a major war within the region, and also due to the imprecise nature of previous empirical studies into its causes. Any of these (or all) three theories advanced above, be it issues under contention, foreign policy reciprocity or power transition, should be able to explain this war and shed light on its causes. Yet none of these leading theories on explaining international action and war causation have been comprehensively applied to the Iran–Iraq War. Furthermore, while previous studies have demonstrated the utility of an integrated approach, they have also fallen short in their systematic examination of this war.

Given the theoretical basis developed above, and the selection of a case for its application, I now turn to the expectations developed from the integrated approach to interstate conflict escalation when applied to the Iran–Iraq War. Each of these different tools utilized as part of the broader integrated approach have three key and interdependent expectations associated with them. Looking first at issues, it is expected that the behavior between these states should first and foremost be issues directed. This leads to the next expectation, which is that the most highly salient issues will direct the interaction between Iran and Iraq during the period under examination. Finally, that these states will seek to resolve these issues through utilizing either conflictual or cooperative foreign policy tools.

## An integrated approach: theoretical foundations 41

It is expected with the utilization of FPR in explaining the causes of this war, that three distinct features should be evident. To begin with, the period preceding the onset of war between Iran and Iraq should be characterized by an escalatory conflict cycle, showing a clear evolution of bilateral relations to war. With a consideration of the issues-based approach, this interaction should be grounded in the contention over highly salient issues.

The next expectation derivative from utilizing FPR is that the bilateral interaction between Iran and Iraq should conform to the basic concept of Axelrod's "tit for tat," with the behavior that each state receives being likewise reciprocated. Consequently, if relations are marked by conflict or cooperation, this should then be sustained in the bilateral interaction between the two states.[45] This will provide support for the existence of reciprocity in the bilateral interactions of states within a dyadic relationship.

The third criterion is that there must be evidence that the nature of change in bilateral relations between Iran and Iraq can be characterized through either growth or decay in that particular behavior—with cooperation and conflict forming either end of the spectrum. This reflects the notion of FPR that relationships should be progressive, with the change shifting towards solidifying a particular type of behavior, or increasingly towards the opposite behavior (either cooperation or conflict), and was founded in the recent study of interstate interaction, reciprocity and conflict escalation by Mark Crescenzi and Andrew Enterline (2001). The issues based approach would also suggest that a change in the behavior between these states would also revolve around the nature of the issues under contention, so it can also be argued that this change should be matched by an evolution or shift in the issues under contention.

Turning to power transition theory, the first expectation is that the period preceding the onset of Iran–Iraq War should demonstrate evidence of a power transition, marked first by a power convergence between these two states, with the initially weaker state reaching parity and then surpassing the power of the initially stronger state (de Soysa *et al.*, 1997). This notion, based on dynamic measures of power, should provide a positive correlation between national power, power transition theory, and the onset of the Iran–Iraq War. At the same time, for this integrated approach to be validated, the states should also be experiencing a reciprocal and escalatory conflict cycle over highly salient issues.

Next, if the comparative power distribution between Iran and Iraq is marked by preponderance, the dyad should be stable and pacific (Lemke, 1997; Sweeney, 2003). Finally, if the dyadic relationship is characterized by parity, conflict should be more likely (Morton and Starr, 2001). These form supplementary parameters to be fulfilled, which if demonstrated, will support the wider framework for power transition theory's explanation of the international interaction between states. It will also provide additional support for the power preponderance theory, and further repudiate the BOP theory.

Taken together, and in summation, these three approaches therefore establish expectations that the period preceding the onset of war between Iran and Iraq will be marked by the evolution of contention over highly salient issues, through a reciprocal and escalatory conflict cycle, and under the conditions of a power convergence and transition. This empirical study is delineated into three distinct phases that are evident in the bilateral relations between Iran and Iraq in the ten years preceding the onset of war—the Pre-Algiers, détente and post-revolution periods. These three periods are distinguished by their homogenous patterns in bilateral relations between Iran and Iraq, stimulated by the contention over distinctive issues, which allow for the delineation and division of their relations.

Phase one, the Pre-Algiers period, began in April 1969 and was marked by the Iranian abrogation of the London Treaty of 1937. The period concluded in March 1975, immediately prior to the Algiers Agreement. These dates signify the beginning and conclusion of an escalatory conflict cycle between Iran and Iraq, in which a process of reciprocal interaction evolved almost to the point of war, with these states contending over the Iranian drive for regional dominance and the Iraqi desire for state consolidation of central authority with the Baathist party. The Pre-Algiers period was distinguishable by a type of interaction—hostile and conflictual—between Iran and Iraq which differentiates itself from the relationship both prior to and subsequent to those dates.

The détente period between Iran and Iraq constitutes the second phase of analysis, beginning with the signing of the Algiers Agreement in March 1975, and concluding with the Iranian revolution in January 1979. Like the Pre-Algiers period, a distinct type of reciprocal behavior characterizes this phase. However, unlike the previous period, the relationship between Iran and Iraq from the Algiers Agreement to the overthrow of the Shah represented a fundamental shift from conflict to cooperation, leading to the normalization of diplomatic relations and cessation of conflict between the two states. This period was also marked by intermittent cooperative moves by each state, and had been stimulated by the removal of contentious and highly salient issues that were evident in the Pre-Algiers period.

The final phase, the post-revolution period, began in February 1979 following the Iranian revolution and the removal of the Shah. It concluded with the onset of the Iran–Iraq War in September 1980. Like the previous two periods, post-revolution relations were characterized by a proclivity towards a certain type of behavior, which was maintained throughout the entire period. At the beginning of this period, however, a distinct shift occurred, with a resumption of hostilities and conflict leading to war as the ultimate result. This was stimulated by the installation of the Iranian revolutionary government, which sought to propagate a Pan-Shi'ism movement within the region, and subsequently formed the key issue under contention from the Iranian side. The Baathist regime in Iraq saw this shift in Iranian policy as a direct threat, leading to the evolution of the other key issue under contention prior to the onset of war in September 1980, which was the overall Iraqi security and survival as an independent functioning state. The next task facing this research is to evaluate these three phases of relations as a focused case study in determining not only the utility of the integrated approach to understanding interstate conflict escalation but also in more thoroughly explaining why the Iran–Iraq War happened when it did.

# 3 The Pre-Algiers period
## Phase 1 of Iran–Iraq relations

The theoretical discussion in Chapter 2 identified the integrated approach to understanding interstate conflict escalation as an appropriate method for examining the Iran–Iraq War. This approach utilizes a multidimensional process to understanding conflict escalation and war, derived from issues under contention, foreign policy reciprocity and power transition theory. In particular, issues were shown to explain what states are likely to fight about, with issue salience the characteristic that most "likely influences the chances for war" (Diehl, 1992: 341). This theory holds that the greater the importance political leaders or publics consign to the issues under contention influences the type of foreign policy behavior enacted. In their examination of territorial issues in the Americas and Western Europe, Hensel and McLaughlin-Mitchell (2005) found that salience levels were a pertinent factor in determining both the escalation of conflict to war and peaceful agreements. Other recent examples have found that issues are an important consideration in the escalation of conflict to war, including Petersen's (2008) examination of regime type and issues under contention, and Rasler and Thompson (2006) who identify issues and rivalry to be important explanatory factors in militarized interstate disputes and war.

Robert Axelrod's (1990) concept of "tit for tat" was also demonstrated to be an appropriate basis for explaining the conflict and war. Building beyond the issues under contention, interstate interaction was shown to be a valuable basis from which to explain the evolution of conflict to war. Indeed, this concept has found resonance within the study of a variety of different conflicts, including Rajimaira's (1997) examination of the enduring conflict between India and Pakistan, and in Goldstein and Pevehouse's (1997) explanation of Serbian actions in the conflict in Bosnia-Herzegovina. As Axelrod (1990: 20) notes, the "tit for tat" strategy is a simple method for explaining the likely behavior of an actor, based on whatever the other actor did on the previous move. Ward and Rajimaira (1992: 345) go beyond Axelrod's initial assertions, suggesting that the concept of reciprocity "can be viewed adequately as a set of norms for behavior . . . [which] represent an underlying level of expected patterns of behavior . . . set[ting] broad parameters for foreign policy interactions."

As a final point, the discussion of power analysis identified A.F.K Organski's (1958) power transition theory as a leading method in measuring the relationship between power and war. This theory holds that conflict is more likely between two states when there has been a convergence and transition in their comparative power position (DiCicco and Levy, 1999). Organski's ideas have been rigorously tested and developed since their inception 50 years ago, with recent examples seen in the work of Sanjian (2003) and Lemke (1997). The link between power transitions and war continues to find support in wide-ranging studies, such as seen in Woosang's (1993: 171) study of Great Power War. He finds that the relationship between power transitions and war can be seen both in the "nineteenth and twentieth centuries . . . [as well as] the pre-1816 period." This link is further supported by Houweling and Siccama (1988: 101), who suggest that "power transitions among great powers are indeed a potent predictor of consecutive outbreak of war."

Assessing the issues under contention and their salience, the foreign policy reciprocity of their interstate interactions, and the dynamic power capabilities of Iran and Iraq enables a researcher to draw several conclusions about the lead up to the war in 1980. First, it will allow the identification of what issues Iran and Iraq were contending over, and the importance of these issues for each country. Second, foreign policy reciprocity analysis will chart the development of the relations between Iran and Iraq, be it conflictual or cooperative, allowing the determination of the existence of patterns in behavior. Third and finally, the assessment of dynamic power capabilities will enable the identification of comparative power capabilities for Iran and Iraq, and the type of change—if any—experienced, and whether this was correlated with the war decision.

This chapter will therefore seek to establish the issues under contention between Iran and Iraq during the Pre-Algiers period (PAP),

46  *The pre-Algiers period*

highlighting the importance of Iranian regional aspirations and Iraqi state consolidation as underlying factors stimulating their interstate interaction. Foreign policy reciprocity will also be utilized to illuminate the evolution of their interstate interaction, including the broadening of stakes in which these issues were played out, up until the point of war in 1975. In doing so, the escalatory and reciprocal nature of their relations will be highlighted, demonstrating context for the evolution of their interaction to war. However, this chapter will conclude by demonstrating the inhibiting force of dynamic power capabilities in the resolution of the issues under contention, with the broadening Iranian power preponderance deterring Iraq from further escalating the conflictual issue resolution.

## Issues under contention: regional dominance and state consolidation

This period was marked by the reciprocal evolution of hostile relations relating to two key underlying issues—Iranian regional dominance and Iraqi state consolidation. These two broad issues are based on a multiplicity of stakes over which Iran and Iraq interacted throughout the period. This includes the disputes over the border delineation on Shatt al Arab waterway, attempts at regional expansion and alliance building, and the external interference in each other's domestic stability.

In 1968, the enunciated British objective to withdraw from the Gulf region by 1971 signaled the beginning of a new defensive (and offensive) strategy for the Shah, with a determined effort aimed at establishing Iranian regional dominance. This was to form the key issue under contention for the Iranians, directing their foreign policy interaction with neighboring states, including Iraq. Clearly articulated in both the Shah's policy statements and foreign policy behavior throughout the Pre-Algiers period, including his stated desire to be the "policeman of the Gulf area" (cited in the *Observer*, 1973), this position was reinforced through the interstate interaction initiated by Iran and their substantial expansion in power capabilities.

Iranian efforts at establishing regional dominance exhibited highly salient intangible and tangible values. On the intangible front, the Shah articulated the prestige that was associated with replacing British protection of the Persian Gulf (PG), stating that Iran was "to present the image of strength, wisdom, and absolutely altruistic purposes" in protecting this region. It was clearly an attempt at not only securing their own defence, but also at elevating perceptions of Iranian influence and status. Their desire for regional dominance also had highly salient tangible values, including maintaining Iranian security and extending their wealth through territorial expansion. First, the impending withdrawal of British troops from the Persian Gulf was viewed by Iran as an opportunity for pro-communist, leftist, or revolutionary forces to move into the region, and was therefore a direct threat to the region's security. The readjustment of their border was to have an impact upon their wealth, with the Iraqis tolling Iranian ships for the right to navigate the Shatt al Arab. One could also argue that the occupation of the three islands in the Persian Gulf allowed for a further extension on Iranian resource possession. The highly salient intangible and tangible values associated with the Iranian pursuit of regional dominance can therefore be categorized as a highly salient issue.

The ruling Baathist party, in contrast to the regional projection seen by the Iranians, was consumed by domestic troubles in securing political legitimacy and control over the Iraqi population. The Iraqi leadership was confronted by a direct threat from three main groups—the Kurdish separatist movement, the Iraqi Shi'ites and the Iraqi Communist Party. Most notable, however, was the aggressive attempts by the Kurdish separatist movement throughout the Pre-Algiers period to establish self-rule and autonomy. The Shah's abrogation of the London treaty seen at the beginning of the period, in addition to the ongoing Iranian power projection and desire for regional dominance, only exacerbated the threat perceptions for Iraqi security and moves towards state consolidation.

Iraqi attempts to consolidate control over their territory had highly salient intangible values associated with it, with both their independent functioning as a state under threat, and their status and influence within the Arab community compromised. The examination of the interstate interaction between Iran and Iraq underscores how the independent functioning of Iraq was undermined by Iranian support for the Kurdish separatist movement as well as their border clashes for control over the Shatt al Arab. Moreover, Iraq's standing within the Arab community and their drive towards being the self-appointed leader of the Arab bloc were damaged by their inability to create and maintain stable control over their own sovereign territory.

Concomitantly, the Iraqi moves towards state consolidation also had important tangible values associated with their overall security and survival. This was demonstrated by the commitment of a large proportion of their military power (over half) dedicated to securing their domestic rule and the survival of a unified and functioning state. The commitment of their military forces to internal security also undermined their ability to confront the challenge faced by the Shah's forceful renegotiation of the London treaty. Obviously the threat to the internal control, in tandem with the external threat faced from Iran, resulted in highly salient tangible values being associated with the Iraqi state consolidation. It could therefore be argued that state consolidation was a highly salient issue overall—with high salience for both tangible and intangible values.

The following discussion on the interstate interaction between Iran and Iraq will now chart the issue evolution and foreign policy reciprocity during this period, identifying the different stakes which these states utilized in attempting to resolve the issues under contention.

## Interstate interaction: hostile reciprocity and conflict spiral

Looking more closely at Iraqi and Iranian interstate interactions, its beginnings were seen in 1969 after a series of border clashes erupted (*Daily Star*, 1975b: 2). In April that year, Iran renounced agreements derived from the 1937 London Treaty (Sirriyeh, 1985; *Washington Post*, 1969: 16) relating to its mutual border with Iraq, which ended the perceived ignominy that the treaty had imposed on Iran, by forcing it to concede territorial rights over the Shatt al-Arab river to Baghdad (*Daily Star*, 1975b: 2). Iran's foreign minister, Khosrow Afshar, announced the abrogation of the treaty, and alleged that continued violations by the Iraqi government, in addition to other acts of aggression, constituted sufficient grounds for its termination (*Washington Post*, 1969: 16). He went further, stating that Iran would "no longer admit anything but an equal distribution of the whole Shatt al Arab according to international principle" (cited in Martin, 1969: 4). Iran had clearly confirmed their determined effort to achieve regional dominance and power projection, with Iraq seeking to maintain their territorial integrity from Iranian aggression.

Iraq responded immediately, moving its military forces to the banks of Shatt al Arab, followed shortly thereafter by Iran (Durdin, 1969).

With their respective forces on the opposing banks, the confrontation escalated. Iranian-flagged ships further punctuated the position of the government in Tehran, continuing to transit the waterway without interference from Iraqi forces (albeit with the protection of the Iranian armed forces, including aerial cover by F-4 fighters) (*Los Angeles Times*, 1969; *New York Times*, 1969a: 10). The refusal of Iranian ships to comply with Iraqi-imposed tolls further heightened the tension.

Iraq's response was to begin forcibly deporting Iranians residing within its borders. Reports emerged of some 10,000 Iranians initially subjected to this treatment, and another 20,000 faced expulsion (Durdin, 1969). Observations were made at the time suggesting that this was the first salvo in the "struggle for influence over the oil-rich Persian Gulf area" brought about by the (then) forthcoming British withdrawal scheduled for 1971 (*Los Angeles Times*, 1969; Karsh, 1987/88).

The impending removal of British troops (and by extension their influence) in the wash-up from the Suez Crisis was seen by Iran as an opening for a leftist, pro-communist, or revolutionary Arab nation, to exert influence within the Persian Gulf (Friendly, 1969: 15; Parasiliti, 2003). It sought to project its own influence within the region, and with this opening move on the Shatt al Arab (to the detriment of Iraq) began pushing towards control of the Persian Gulf. The Shah (cited in Friendly, 1969: 15) clarified the position of his government within the region, suggesting that

> [w]hen the British leave Iran can do it, because we have no territorial or colonial designs. Iran's role in the Gulf is to present the image of strength, wisdom, and absolutely altruistic purposes, and yet without any thought of trying to play Big Daddy.

Iran also repeatedly made clear its dissatisfaction with the situation on the Shatt al Arab, reporting to the UN that it required a more equitable solution to the current border question before hostilities could be defused (*New York Times*, 1969b: 10). The ongoing reports of Iraqi mistreatment of Iranians within its border only served to further agitate the situation between the two countries (Durdin, 1969).

In September 1969, relations between the two countries deteriorated further when reports emerged of Iranian support for the Kurdish movement in Iraq. Iranian military forces were attacked as they moved across the border (30 troops were killed, while 14 were captured), with Iraq contending that these troops were part of a unit created to aid the Kurdish autonomous movement in Northern Iraq (*New York Times*, 1969c: 13). The surviving Iranian troops were paraded on Iraqi television (*Washington Post*, 1969: 10).

Iran denied these reports. A Foreign Ministry spokesman suggested that it was more likely that they were simply Iranian Kurds who had decided to join their 'brother' Kurds in their struggle against the Iraqi government (*Washington Post*, 1969: 10). The capture of these troops was, nevertheless, seen as proof of a broadening conflict emerging between Iran and Iraq (*Christian Science Monitor*, 1970). Indeed, before long the Iraqi government reciprocated the Iranian moves, instituting a propaganda campaign seeking to incite a similar Kurdish movement within Iran (*New York Times*, 1970b: 8).

The tense atmosphere continued into 1970, with Iraq claiming that Iran had supported an attempted coup against the Iraqi Baathist regime. This served as a pretext for the Iranian ambassador and four other diplomats to be ejected from Iraq (*Chicago Tribune*, 1970).[1] In addition to diplomatic expulsions, Iraq also closed three Iranian consulates (Cooley, 1970). Iran promptly reciprocated these actions, closing Iraqi consulates and expelling the Iraqi ambassador (Cooley, 1970). These moves reflected the accelerating polarization of the relations between Iran and Iraq, particularly in terms of the future of the Persian Gulf (Cooley, 1970).[2]

In an attempt to portray Iran as an outsider in the region statements were increasingly released by the Baathist leadership relating to Iraq's interests in the Gulf region, and its desire to maintain the 'Arab character' of the area (*New York Times*, 1970b: 8). By July 1970, Iraqi president Ahmed Hassan al Bakr was pushing for the establishment of a Gulf security pact to protect against what it saw as imperialist expansionism by Iran (*New York Times*, 1970d: 11; *New York Times*, 1970b: 8). Iran, for its part, continued its own push towards establishing a security pact (with Saudi Arabia), and reinforced its stance in the Gulf by stating that it was "both willing and able to protect [its] interests" (cited in Izzard, 1970: 4).

Relations markedly deteriorated in 1971, when Iranian military forces took control over three islands within the Persian Gulf. This event came one day prior to the completion of British security obligations to the Trucial States[3] (which were to later become the United Arab Emirates), and saw an Iranian task force landing troops simultaneously on Abu Musa, and the Greater and Lesser Tunbs in the Strait of Hormuz.[4]

The occupation of Abu Musa occurred without incident, but the landing on the two Tunbs islands, over which the Ras al Khaimah's (the Trucial state formally in control of these islands) ruler had refused to negotiate, resulted in a skirmish with local security forces. Iranian forces quickly overwhelmed the opposition, although a Ras al Khaimah security member and three Iranians were killed (IISS, 1971; Parasiliti, 2003).

The immediate reaction by Arab states was a volley of protest led by Iraq, acting in a role where Baghdad saw itself as the "self-appointed leader of progressive forces in the Gulf" (IISS, 1971: 40). Iraq subsequently broke off diplomatic relations with Iran and the UK,[5] and began urging other Arab countries to do likewise (*Daily Star*, 1971b: 1). Continuing a process that had been ongoing over the previous two years, Iraq further utilized the large Iranian expatriate community residing within its borders as a means by which to illustrate its displeasure with Iran, not only harassing Iranians within Iraq but also undertaking a program of mass deportations.[6] This was despite posturing by Saddam Hussein (cited in Cooley, 1972: 21) that "the foreigners who were expelled violated national and international laws" and that these "measures" had been undertaken without regard to race.

The Iranian expatriate colony within Southern Iraq was seen as one of the key areas for Iraq to "strike back" at Iran, described aptly by Marvine Howe (1972: 6) as the "pawns in a power game" between Tehran and Baghdad. Accusations also surfaced from the Baathist regime that Tehran was using the community as a "fifth column," seeking to undermine Iraq's authority (Howe, 1972).

Hence, the occupation of the Hormuz islands, although not a direct act against the sovereignty of Iraq, was perceived and interpreted as a threat to the overall security of the state and as a direct threat to Iraq's own goals within the Gulf region. From the beginning of 1969, following the Iranian abrogation of the 1937 London Treaty, Iraq had vocalized its desire for a greater role within the Gulf. To this end, it had sought to create a security pact within the region, and had established an increasingly friendly relationship with Bahrain, one of the islands within the Gulf that was subject to claims by Iran (Martin, 1970). Iraq's forced dislocation of Iranian residents residing within Iraqi borders, in tandem with its diplomatic initiatives with Arab states against the occupation, were thus a reciprocal response to the threat it felt from Iran and its occupation of the three islands in the Gulf.

In this way, Iraq's moves were reflective of contingent reciprocity. Baghdad's actions displayed their displeasure at the moves by Tehran within the Strait of Hormuz, while not requiring it to correspondingly occupy contentious territory. By undertaking the actions that it did, Baghdad responded to Tehran's behavior in a similar manner, and as a result continued to conform to the underlying assumptions of reciprocity theorists (Keohane, 1987).

Iran, in turn, reciprocated Iraqi actions by drawing international attention to the plight of Iranian citizens within Iraq, hosting press conferences and even tours for foreign correspondents of refugee camps, which contained many of the victims of the Iraqi deportation (*Daily Star*, 1972c: 1). The Iranian government also mobilized domestic opposition against Iraq through strikes, protests, and extensive debate within the Iranian Lower House of Parliament (*Daily Star*, 1972a: 3).

Iranian religious leaders were especially active in advocating nationwide strikes to highlight their opposition to Iraq's treatment of Iranians, particularly as the abuse was aimed at Shiite Muslims in southern Iraq. The capital, Tehran, was the focal point. A half-day strike on January 5, 1972, culminated in the closure of stores throughout the city, enabling the community to express its protest, which included the collection of grievance registers at local mosques (*Daily Star*, 1972a: 3).

For its part, Iran's Lower House of Parliament issued a series of press releases condemning what it classified a directed 'campaign' against Iran, with the "maltreatment and mass expulsion of Iranians" (*Daily Star*, 1972a: 3). Public statements from leading Iranian parliamentary members also criticized the "Baathist regime for its actions against Iranians in Jarbala and Narjaf districts, [and] urged world nations to assist in halting Iraq's 'behavior' towards Iranians" (*Daily Star*, 1972a: 3). The Shah (cited in Howe, 1972: 6) also publicly denounced the actions by Iraq, suggesting that Iraq could "only go so far in the policy of provocations" before it reached a "point it can no longer be accepted."

Clearly each state was reciprocating the actions of the other, or as Axelrod argues, conforming to the simple strategy of "tit for tat." Moreover, it remains evident that these states continued to contend over the two principal issues identified at the beginning of the period, with the Iranian desire to establish regional dominance and Iraq seeking to consolidate and secure their domestic authority. The year 1972 proved to be no different, with the beginning of the year marked by a series of border clashes between Iraqi and Iranian military forces (*New York Times*, 1972c: 3; *Washington Post*, 1972: 13). The year 1972 also saw the continuation of Iraqi attempts to consolidate an 'Arab front' against Iran, with a diplomatic mission led by Iraqi foreign minister Said Abdul Baghi touring the Gulf States (*New York Times*, 1972c: 3).

The beginning of 1973 was marked by continued clashes on the border between Iran and Iraq (*Chicago Tribune*, 1973; *Washington Post*, 1973: 18). In March 1973, however, Iraq's focus shifted temporarily to its focus on to the border with Kuwait, where a skirmish occurred between their respective military forces. Taking place at a time in which both states were involved in border delineation talks,[7] the outcome was the subsequent occupation of the Kuwaiti border area by Iraq (*New York Times*, 1973: 6). This demonstrated the ongoing battle facing Iraqi authorities in securing and maintaining their territorial boundaries.

Iranian involvement was maintained in this unfolding conflict, with the Shah immediately offering support to the Kuwaitis to repel Iraqi aggression (IISS, 1973). Although the offer was refused (Kuwait also feared the intentions of Iran) it continued to reflect the hostile nature of the bilateral relations between these two neighbors (IISS, 1973). Every action by one state was subsequently reciprocated by the other state. The degree to which the behavior was reciprocated, although not exacting in its equivalence, reflected the general precepts of contingent reciprocity.

The actions of Iran demonstrated its desire within the Gulf region to become the major player establishing, projecting, and directing the relations among neighboring countries, including Iraq (Karsh, 1987/88; Mehrawari, 1973; *Observer*, 1973). The Shah (cited in the *Observer*, 1973) further punctuated his vision for the region, explicitly stating 'I am the policeman of the Gulf area'. The Shah articulated this vision through explicit actions, including extending the offer of aid (both financial and militarily) to neighboring states. One such example was seen throughout the beginning of the period in Oman, where the Shah deployed some 3000 troops (Ottaway, 1973; Scott-Plummer, 1973).

These troops were located in the southernmost province of Dhofar, and sought to counter the threat posed by leftist guerrillas supported by the Peoples Republic of South Yemen and their Soviet backers (Ottaway, 1973; *Daily Star*, 1975g: 2; *Financial Times*, 1974).

The Shah sought to further establish his position, utilizing not only Iran's rapidly expanding military forces but also diplomatic collaboration (Howe, 1972). This was particularly the case with regard to control over the Strait of Hormuz, which continued to be a focus in Iran's power positioning. Tentative moves were made to form a security partnership with Oman in order to enable control over the entry of shipping into the Persian Gulf (Ottaway, 1973). Although this plan was meant to reflect the dual purpose of preventing arms being shipped to dissidents operating in the area (and notionally controlling environmental pollution), it primarily reflected Iran's security preoccupations (Ottaway, 1973), demonstrating another step in Iran's plans to control the Persian Gulf area, looking beyond the Hormuz Straits towards its main entry point to the Indian Ocean.

Iran also made use of diplomatic statements enunciating support for the security of surrounding countries such as Saudi Arabia and the United Arab Emirates. An example of this occurred during a visit to London by Iranian premier Amir Abbas Hoveyda, who openly stated Iran's position regarding Gulf security by stressing that "Iran would not permit any 'subversive' activity in the region" (cited in Melloan, 1973: 26). Iran also maintained friendly relations and commercial links (particularly through the supply of petroleum) with Israel under the Shah, despite its continued support for Arab states in their campaign to liberate the Palestinians (Weinraub, 1973: 2; Howe, 1972: 6; Melloan, 1973).

Many of the statements regarding Iran's desires within the Gulf region were also influenced by Iraq, which, as Premier Hoveyda (cited in de Onis, 1973: 3) stated, was "directing a campaign of sabotage, infiltration and hostile propaganda against Iran." Iraq, for its part, demonstrated this with ongoing calls for both the Arab and Baluchi minorities to rebel against Iranian central authority (de Onis, 1973).

In spite of Iranian and Iraqi relations being characterized by conflict to this point, the 1973 October war between the Arab states and Israel resulted in a temporary interruption. Iraq announced its wish "to participate in [the] battle together with [its] Arab brethren."[8] Iraqi participation was contingent upon securing its eastern border. Yet even this was characterized by patterns of reciprocity, given that the Baathist regime recognized that a quiescent entr'acte to the conflict with Iran was needed. One day into the Arab–Israeli war, Iran and Iraq restored diplomatic relations, allowing Iraq to concentrate its support for Arabs (*Daily Star*, 1975b: 2). With the temporary respite, Iraq was also able to redistribute two divisions from its eastern border with Iran, notionally to support Syria (*Daily Star*, 1975b: 2).

Following the Arabs' swift defeat at the hands of the Israelis,[9] relations between Iran and Iraq quickly reverted to the conflict cycle evident since 1969.[10] Within two months border skirmishes were again reported, and quickly escalated throughout the beginning of 1974.[11] February 1974 saw the most significant engagements between Iran and Iraq, with reports of the two sides extensively employing armored vehicles, heavy artillery, and aerial support.[12] Mutual recriminations were made by each side about who was the aggressor, and how much damage was inflicted upon the opposing side. It was, however, recognized by both sides that there were at least 150 casualties in the fighting.[13]

The conflict continued on into March, during which time the Iranians reaffirmed their support for the Kurdish separatist movement in Iraq, and gave assurances of full support for their struggle against the Baathist regime (Roberts, 1975). This came in the form of both material and moral support, removing boundaries to the flow of goods and weapons to the Kurdish rebellion, and supplying the guerrillas with important heavy artillery support in the form of 42 155 mm heavy artillery pieces. These offered a much-needed force supplement to the mobile Kurdish forces, which up to that point had lacked armor or heavy weaponry (Karsh, 1987/88; Roberts, 1975; *Daily Star*, 1975h: 2).

Even a cease-fire brokered by the United Nations Security Council (Winder, 1974), which sought to remove the concentrations of Iranian and Iraqi armed forces along the entire border, failed to defuse the conflict. Both sides continued to add to an extensive list of infringements by the opposing party throughout the remainder of 1974. Examples ranged from "premeditated and treacherous" attacks by the Iranian forces in August,[14] to the dropping of bombs on "defenseless villages" by Iraqi military aircraft in September,[15] and the recurrent "acts of aggression" by Iranian forces against Iraq throughout October.[16]

The claims and counter-claims were covered extensively by the international press, although a clear picture of what was transpiring between the two states was difficult to discern, mainly because coverage was directed by state-owned media organs. Typical of propaganda, it was portrayed in such a way to positively reflect the actions of the regime, and depict the opposing side as the instigator.

It was surprising then, that the period concluded with the introduction of the Algiers Agreement in March 1975. Signaling the end to hostilities, the Shah of Iran and the vice-president of Iraq, Saddam Hussein, met in Algiers to broker an agreement which sought to stem the ongoing conflict between the two countries (Parasiliti, 2003; *Daily Star*(a), 1975: 2). It came at a time when the reciprocal conflict between the two states had almost evolved to the point of war. Indeed, the significance of this agreement was palpable to Saddam Hussein (cited in Hoagland, 1975: 16), who stated, "A war between Iran and us was almost on the point of occurring, that was all too clear to us and to Iran. Neither party wanted war; both decided for peace."

The Pre-Algiers period clearly shows that a reciprocal "tit for tat" scenario marked the relationship between Iran and Iraq up until March 1975. Bilateral interaction emerging from the Iranian abrogation of the London Treaty through to the border skirmishes in 1974 all resonate with Axelrod's claim that states will reciprocate the behavior they receive. The issues under contention were both classified as highly salient for Iran and Iraq, and were demonstrated to play out across a number of different stakes during the period. Even Saddam Hussein recognized that the two states had reciprocally escalated their conflict to the point where war seemed inevitable.

Yet the states stopped short of war, with relations experiencing a sudden reversal in March 1975 with the signing of the Algiers Agreement. The result was a cooperative end to the hostilities and conflict between the two nations. This sudden change, I argue, was influenced by the comparative power position of Iran and Iraq. Although both these states had followed a process of interactive and reciprocal escalation in trying to resolve the issues under contention, it was the relative power capabilities that clearly influenced the decision not to resort to war. While Iran enjoyed broad superiority in its comparative power position, war was simply not an option for Iraq. I demonstrate this further below.

## Dynamic power distribution: broadening Iranian power preponderance

In examining the comparative power capabilities of Iran and Iraq, I begin with demographic indicators, as they offer the broadest classification of a state's capabilities, and remain a central basis for most assessments of national power (Singer *et al.*, 1972). I will then move on to an examination of the other two key bases for determining national power—economic and military capabilities. Finally, the analysis will conclude with demonstrating the reinforcing nature of the two power conversion factors—military modernization and absorption, and social stability—in augmenting the Iranian power divergence and broad preponderance over Iraq.

### *Demographic indicators: Iranian superiority*

Looking first at demographic indicators, we see that data relating to total population shows Iran was able to maintain a clear superiority over Iraq for the entire Pre-Algiers period. Iraq, however, was able to narrow the gap slightly from the 1970 level at 3.04:1, to 2.95:1 in 1975.[17] This was as a result of a sustained higher growth rate for the period, averaging an annual increase of 3.33 percent to Iran's 2.71 percent.[18] The Pre-Algiers period finished with Iran maintaining a clear superiority with an advantage of 2.95:1 over Iraq.

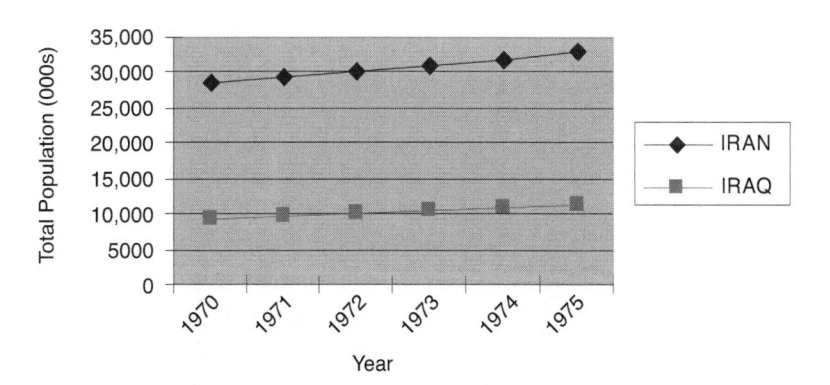

*Figure 3.1* Pre-Algiers total population.

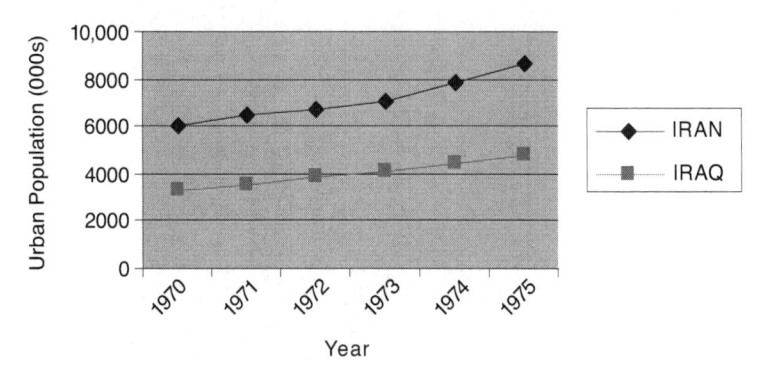

*Figure 3.2* Pre-Algiers urban population.

Changes in urban population patterns show a similar result. Iran maintained clear superiority over Iraq during the entire period. Iraq was again able to narrow the gap slightly, maintaining a higher average annual increase at 8 percent, in contrast to Iran with 7.5 percent.[19] Despite this higher annual average, Iran showed signs of an emerging rapid expansion of urban population, with 1974 and 1975 experiencing growth of 11.5 percent and 10.3 percent, respectively.[20] Sustained increases by Iraq were able to mitigate these large Iranian increases, yet Iran maintained broad superiority, with a 1.79:1 advantage over Iraq.[21]

Consequently, demographic indicators suggest that Iran was able to maintain in broad measure a clear advantage over Iraq for the Pre-Algiers period. This was evidenced by a total population almost three times greater than Iraq, and an urban population 1.79 times greater.

## Economic capabilities: initial divergence and Iranian superiority

A review of economic capabilities reveals that based on its first measure, Gross Domestic Product (GDP), Iran was able to extend a clear lead over Iraq throughout the Pre-Algiers period. Iran saw its comparative advantage peak in 1972, when its GDP had expanded to a ratio of 6:1 over Iraq.[22] Iraq was able to close the gap somewhat after 1972, with a substantially higher average annual growth rate of 14.2 percent (as compared with Iran at 6.9 percent).[23] Nevertheless, Iran's advantage was extended overall as it experienced a higher average for the entire

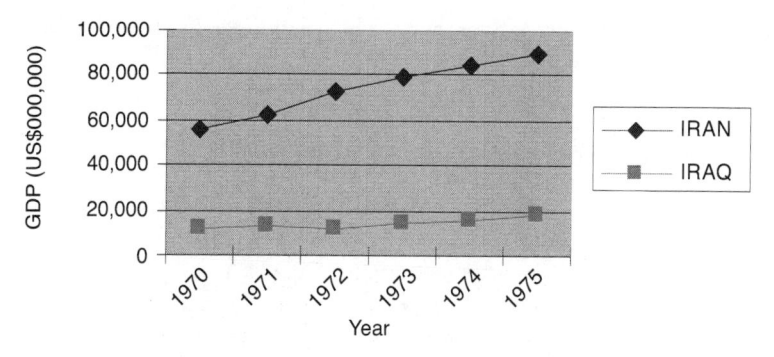

*Figure 3.3* Pre-Algiers GDP.

Pre-Algiers period, at 9.85 percent (compared with Iraq, with 9.14 percent).[24] Iran finished this period with GDP superiority over Iraq at some 4.93:1.

Data relating to GDP Per Capita also supports the supposition that Iran was able to extend its superiority over Iraq during the Pre-Algiers period. Like raw GDP, Iran saw its greatest lead over Iraq in 1972, when its GDP Per Capita advantage extended to 2:1.25. Iraq was, however, able to narrow the gap slightly, through a higher average growth rate—10.5 percent, compared with 4 percent after 1972.[26] Even so, Iran finished the period with a GDP Per Capita advantage of 1.67:1 over Iraq.

Indicators relating to economic capabilities thus complement the initial conclusion drawn from demographic indicators, suggesting that Iran was actually able to augment its superiority over Iraq from 1970–75. Stronger overall growth by Iran in both economic indices enabled Iran

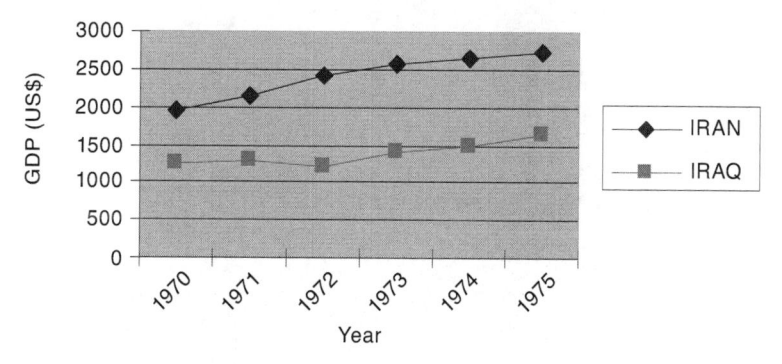

*Figure 3.4* Pre-Algiers GDP per capita.

60  *The pre-Algiers period*

to experience a power divergence. This made war in 1975 a dubious proposition for Baghdad.

**Military power: further divergence and Iranian superiority**

The first military power measure, military expenditure, indicates Iran was able to experience a comparative power divergence in relation to Iraq in the Pre-Algiers period. Although Iraq was able to narrow the gap in 1971, where the comparative ratio closed from an Iranian advantage of 2.9:1 to 1.72:1, this was largely due to Iranian expenditure stabilizing during that year.[27] Thereafter Iran was able to consistently extend its lead as a result of a higher average annual growth, at 63 percent as compared with Iraq's 50 percent.[28] Both states experienced considerable overall growth, with Iranian and Iraqi expenditures increasing 807 percent and 533 percent respectively.[29] The period concluded with Iran dramatically enhancing its initial advantage of 2.92:1 to an impressive 4.19:1 over Iraq.[30]

A comparison of military personnel figures indicates Iraq experienced a slight convergence with Iran from 1970–75. Iran nevertheless maintained general superiority through the entire period. The Iraqi convergence was stimulated by a major rise in 1975, when Iraqi personnel levels increased by 41 percent.[31] It was by far the highest growth experienced by either country (with Iran peaking at 24 percent), and lifted Iraq's average annual growth in military personnel to 11.2 percent as

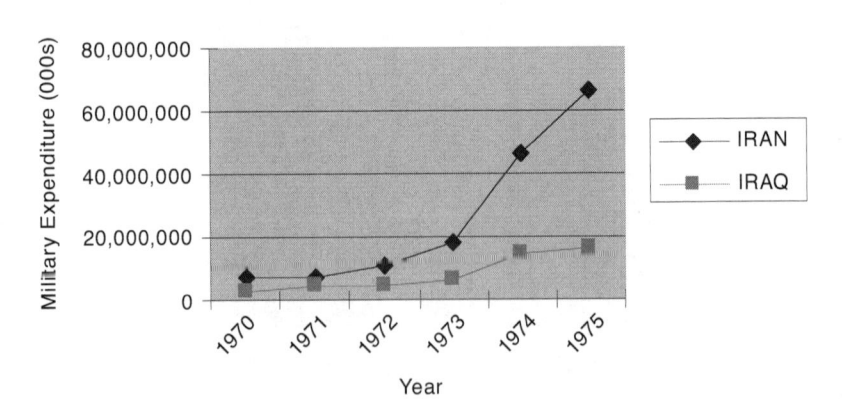

*Figure 3.5* Pre-Algiers military expenditure.

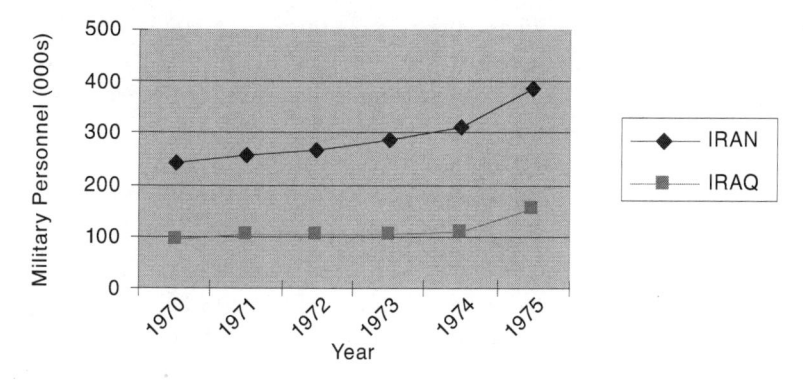

*Figure 3.6* Pre-Algiers military personnel.

compared with 9.7 percent for Iran.[32] Yet Iran's advantage of 2.5:1 over Iraq underlined its lead in this area.

Thus, although Iraq experienced a slight convergence in relation to military personnel levels it did not seriously challenge Iranian superiority. Military expenditure data further confirms this, with Tehran achieving significant comparative increases over Iraq given that its spending reached over four times the amount committed by Baghdad. These figures reinforce the conclusion that Iran was clearly more powerful than Iraq from 1970–75, and suggest that it may have in fact attained greater divergence in its comparative power capabilities during the period.

## Military modernization and absorption: continued Iranian superiority

Military modernization and absorption, a critical power conversion factor in the latter part of the 1970s, did not adversely affect the introduction of Iranian or Iraqi military material in the Pre-Algiers period. Looking first at Iran, their military modernization process was characterized by a major build-up throughout the beginning of the period with advanced aircraft, anti-aircraft weaponry, naval infrastructure, ships, and army equipment and training (Mehrawari, 1973). An indication of the degree to which the Iranians concentrated on modernization was the US$18,000 million it spent in just five years (Marks, 1977).[33]

This was a reasonably smooth process through to 1975 as the two key services, the air force and army, augmented their capabilities.[34] Although beginning the period with arguably the most advanced fighter aircraft in the region including five squadrons (80 aircraft) of F5 tactical fighter bombers, two squadrons (32 a/c) of F-4D all weather fighter-bombers, and 20 F-86 all-weather interceptors (IISSa, 1970/71: 39), the Iranians pushed forward with a process of phasing out older aircraft. In 1971, the process began with a phasing out of older aircraft, expanding their more advanced fighters with the order of 32 F-4E (IISSb, 1971/1972: 28). The year 1972 saw the expansion of F5 fighter squadrons to six; with the complete phase-out of older F-86 all weather fighters (IISSb, 1971/72: 31) and 1973 saw a rapid expansion of the air force with both F-4E (70) and F-5E (141) ordered in large numbers. By 1975 these figures had expanded to 10 squadrons with 80 F-5A and 45 F-5E's (IISSd, 1974/75: 33).

The Iranian army began the 1970s with a modest number of armored divisions, with two divisions expanded to three by following year. The year 1972 also marked the initial delivery of the 800 ordered Chieftain tanks which were increasingly phased into service expanding their tank and land warfare capabilities. By 1974 some 300 Chieftains were beginning to draw level with the M-47 (400) and M-60A1 (460).

On the other hand, the Iranian navy, although experiencing some growth, experienced a much more moderate expansion. The relative personnel figures of the Iranian navy remained the same at the beginning of the 1970s, maintaining a limited number of destroyers, frigates and corvettes. However, over the period it expanded to three destroyers, four frigates (with the latest Seakiller SSM and Seacat SAM), and four corvettes (IISSd, 1973/74: 32).

The process of force modernization was also extensively assisted by foreign personnel, especially from its main arms supplier, the US (IISS, 1976; Marks, 1977). This allowed for a more rapid integration of the advanced military hardware into a less sophisticated military force, particularly in terms of the progressive modernization of the Iranian air force, which was still adapting to the phase out of obsolete fighter aircraft and introduction of much more advanced fighters such as the F-5Es.

Iraq also actively engaged in a process of force modernization, although its achievements were more modest than Iran's, with a more moderated and drawn out introduction of newer military hardware. The implementation of the treaty of Friendship and Cooperation with the *Union of Soviet Socialist Republics* (USSR) in 1972 brought with it the opportunity to purchase new Soviet arms.[35] This was particularly the case with both the army and air force, which saw the introduction of the T-54/55 tank and MiG-21. The end of the period also saw an agreement being reached between Iraq and the USSR for the delivery of MiG-23 fighters (IISSe, 1974/75: 90).

The analysis of military modernization suggests a further solidification in Iranian power superiority that was also evident in relation to the demographic, economic, and military indicators discussed above. Iran was able to support its major arms build-up undertaken in the Pre-Algiers period with extensive foreign assistance. The Iraqi process of development was assisted by the USSR, but it was rather more limited. The two therefore encountered no power conversion issues associated with force modernization and the subsequent absorption of military material.

*Social stability: clear Iranian superiority*

While the Iranian armed forces were able to concentrate on modernization during the early 1970s, Iraq experienced significant domestic difficulties in the form of the renewed Kurdish guerrilla movement (*Daily Star*, 1974d: 6). Baathist policy sought to resolve the internal conflict with the Kurds, utilizing a "part-reconciliation, part-annihilation" policy to deal attempts to gain greater autonomy (*Daily Star*, 1974d: 6). Originating from perceived weaknesses in the central government's authority following the revolution in 1958, the Kurds had progressively pushed for greater autonomy from the Sunni Arab dominated central authority. The movement, however, was located in a critical area with valuable oil reserves and facilities important for maintaining the power of the government. Attempts at repression in the early 1960s had resulted in sporadic heavy fighting between the armed forces and Kurdish separatists (*Daily Star*, 1975h: 2).

Although a partial truce was reached in 1970, the following three years saw intermittent clashes as Baghdad and the Kurds attempted to develop an acceptable formula for self-rule. Reports emerged of ongoing and intermittent clashes between the two sides as temporary measures were instituted for the expanded Kurdish autonomy agreement that had been reached in 1970.[36] The Kurdish guerrilla movement experienced a significant revival in 1974 following the rejection of a proposed autonomy plan by the central Baathist regime (*Daily Star*, 1975d: 2). It was reported that following this event, some 48,000 Iraqi army personnel, in the form of three divisions, moved into the predominantly Kurdish areas of Kirkuk, Erbil, and Sulaimaniya (*Washington Post*, 1974: 16; Clarity, 1974: 4).[37] This was a significant proportion of Iraqi servicemen (accounting for nearly half its entire manpower),[38] and thus absorbing much of its military capacity, with the effect of redirecting the Iraqi armed forces from external threats to internal security duties.

The beginning of 1970 also saw Iraq confronting economic problems caused by widespread labor shortages in urban areas, and the product of a substantial percentage of the population still committed to the agricultural sector. It was still faced with the issue of being unable to fill all employment vacancies, especially in the skilled sector.[39] According to the Iraqi minister for planning, Dr. Hashem, agricultural production accounted for some 70 percent of the work force, and yet it only produced a third of Iraq's income (Schmidt, 1970: 3).

Workforce distribution became a pertinent issue actively dealt with in government policies. Increasingly the manipulation of training and education was undertaken to produce what the economy required (*Daily Star*, 1971a: 3). In 1970, Dr. Hashem implemented widespread manpower relocation programs to shift the rural segment of the workforce, which included the installation of computers to assist in agricultural management (Schmidt, 1970: 3). The Baath regime also utilized collective farms and cooperatives, which emphasized the use of mechanized production, to assist the workforce shift, overcoming subsequent shortages in the rural sector (Howe, 1971: 2). This obviously impacted upon their ability to translate available resources within Iraq, and particularly human resources, into actualized economic power capabilities.

Conversely, during the Pre-Algiers period the Shah's authoritarian rule was able to control competing opposition groups with what was described as 'one of the most extensive and efficient police forces in the world' (Marks, 1977: 1).[40] One such example was during the institution of the White Revolution (an initiative launched by the Shah to stimulate domestic growth and development)[41] during which all opposition was suppressed through the use of force. An estimated 200 anti-reform agitators and guerrillas were executed or killed in clashes (Vis Raein, 1973). The Shah also closed 95 percent of Iranian newspapers in late 1974 to control criticism of the regime, with the remaining papers controlled more aggressively by the state (Housego, 1975). Even attempts to reinvigorate political discourse were halted (including the temporary introduction of a second political party), after the Shah conveniently "took exception to attacks made by the party on the budget the Government [had] presented" (Housego, 1975: 4).

In addition to the maintenance of tight control over the political environment within Iran, the basic modernization program implemented by the Shah was able to boost literacy rates amongst the impoverished and uneducated, and thereby resulted in the intellectual and social empowerment of both the urban and rural populace. One such method that was utilized by the Shah to rectify the high illiteracy rates in Iran was the "Literacy Corps."[42] According to Raein (1973: 3) the Literacy Corps was able to lower the illiteracy rate in Iran from some 80 percent in 1963 to 50 percent in 1973. It did so by redirecting high school graduates away from compulsory military service to the Literacy Corps, who were sent to rural villages to set up basic education programs in writing, reading, and arithmetic.[43] Lieberman (1979: 295) argues that beyond this empowerment of social groups through the easing of restrictions, the rural mass was able to articulate its desire for more freedom and access to resources through its increasing education.

So while both societies experienced significant rural-to-urban migration during the beginning of the 1970s, with each implementing education policies to attempt to manipulate and develop this shift from rural to urban dwelling, it was Iran that was able to initially capitalize on the forcèd integration of its social changes. By the end of the period, Iraq had begun to experience shortages, both in skilled labor in the urban areas, and in manual labor in outlying rural areas (Morris, 1977: 18; Cockburn, 1977).

Comparative patterns of social stability thus reconfirms the process of divergence evident in the comparative power positions of Iran and Iraq, with Iran extending its overall power advantage. The Kurdish guerrilla movement was particularly obstructive in that it required the extensive attention of the Iraqi military. The Kurds comprised a sizeable element of the total population and efforts to quell their rebellion removed an estimated 10–20 percent from Iraq's potential GDP.[44]

## Highly salient issues in a conflict spiral: a peaceful conclusion?

In concluding the analysis of the Pre-Algiers period, it is clear to see how the two issues under contention—Iranian regional dominance and Iraqi state consolidation—evolved through a reciprocal conflict cycle to the point of war in 1975. It was at this point, however, when it appeared that war was inevitable, that power capabilities became a real inhibiting force. Iraq simply did not have the capabilities to escalate conflict over these issues further, since Iranian superiority had expanded throughout the period. Equally, Iran's preponderant power position enabled it to articulate and attain its goals with regard to border disputes, and facilitating the regional projection of its power without the need to resort to war.

The power disparities between the two states were reflected in the Algiers Agreement. Far-reaching concessions were made by the Iraqis to finally resolve the conflict and end the domestic instability created by the Iranian support for the Kurds. Perhaps the most contentious Iraqi capitulation was the delineation of the Shatt al Arab in accordance with the Thalweg line.[45] This benefited Iran by reinforcing its initial claims to shared control of the river, following its abrogation of the London Treaty in 1969,[46] and shifting the mutual border in favor of Iran (*Daily Star*, 1974c: 1). In return, the Iranians retracted their support for the Kurdish guerrilla movement in Iraq, and agreed to establish further security patrols on their mutual border to prevent Kurdish elements infiltrating into Iraq (*Daily Star*, 1974c: 1; *Daily Star*, 1975b: 2).

So while the issues under contention and the interstate interaction between the two states demonstrate the reciprocal and conflictual escalation of their relations to the point of war in 1975, highlighting the most salient issues that these states fighting over, the 'final step' in resorting to war was not taken due to the inhibiting force of the power between the two states. Viewing power transition in the context of this broader conflict cycle also demonstrates the discrete phases in the Iran–Iraq relationship, and offers more clarity and context than simply focusing on material capability changes over the period. Power transition theory only elucidates the fact that a divergence had occurred in comparative capabilities but does not account for the conflict that was occurring between Iran and Iraq from 1969 to 1975. Issues under contention and foreign policy reciprocity, for their part, demonstrate what the states were fighting about and how the relationship was characterized by conflict and reciprocity, but cannot explain why war was not pursued in seeking the resolution of these issues. Taken together, however, these instruments highlight the value of an integrated approach to explaining this conflict.

# 4 The détente period

## Phase 2 of Iran–Iraq relations

This chapter explores the second phase of Iran–Iraq relations, the détente period, applying the integrated approach to understanding interstate conflict escalation. In doing so, it will be demonstrated how this period experienced cooperative reciprocity towards Iranian regional leadership, initiatives for regional security cooperation, and economic collaboration around petroleum prices. Cooperative foreign policy reciprocity evolved throughout the period, including with the backdrop of the Iranian revolution. Indeed, the Iraqi government even sought to mitigate the domestic instability seen in Iran by supporting the Shah's request to eject prominent revolutionary leader Ayatollah Khomeini. It will be demonstrated that this cooperation took place in spite of the rapid convergence that was experienced in the comparative dynamic power capabilities of Iran and Iraq, although the greatest level of cooperation was seen under Iranian preponderance at the beginning of the period.

### Issues under contention: issue resolution and economic issues

Relations in the détente period were marked by the dramatic shift from conflict to cooperation seen with the implementation of the Algiers Agreement, leading to the normalization of diplomatic relations and cessation of conflict between the two states. The interstate interaction between these two countries continued to be based on the solidification of Iraqi domestic control and Iranian regional dominance; however, it was no longer characterized by competition and conflictual interaction.

As discussed in the previous chapter, the principal issue underlying Iranian interaction with Iraq was the highly salient drive for regional

*The détente period* 69

dominance. This continued to provide the backdrop for their interaction over the period. The Algiers Agreement demonstrated Iraqi acquiescence to Iranian demands with the positive delineation of their shared border towards Iran—and the completion of their competition over the Iranian drive for regional dominance. For its part, Iran was willing to restrict their intervention in the domestic affairs of Iraq—and in particular, the military support of the Kurdish separatist movement—which allowed the Baathist party to quickly remove this threat to their security. The examination of Iranian–Iraqi interaction will also highlight the shift that occurred away from Iraqi "Arab-based" balancing of Iranian power projection, towards the cooperative drive for security agreements over the Persian Gulf region, further reinforcing the perception of Iranian regional dominance.

Likewise, the Baathist preoccupation with securing their legitimacy and control their territory saw their willingness in the Algiers Agreement to concede sovereignty over the Shatt al Arab waterway to the Thalweg line. After which point the Baathist regime implemented a swift and decisive military campaign against the Kurdish separatist movement. This provided the backdrop to further cooperative moves with Iran throughout the period, including the ejection of Ayatollah Khomeini from Najaf in 1978 at the behest of the Shah.

The cooperative moves by the two states also resulted in a common economic response to the issue of petroleum prices. Forming a moderately salient issue for both states, the Saudi Arabian led split in OPEC regulated petroleum prices threatened these state's wealth, security and influence in the international community. On the tangible side, both Iran and Iraq utilized large proportions of their oil revenues in the development of their military forces and economic well-being of their subjects, which reinforced their rule and overall domestic stability. The price split led to a two-tier pricing structure, undermining their overall sales and income from petroleum. The division of OPEC's authority and pre-eminence in setting oil prices internationally was also diminished by the Saudi moves, which clearly split the power of the group offering a cheaper price.

Thus, with the Algiers Agreement resolving the highly contentious issues evident in the previous period, and the cooperative moves towards security issues, relations between these states stabilized for the period. As noted above, the one point during the period where a common issue

70  *The détente period*

emerged (OPEC pricing), these states demonstrated their willingness to cooperate. With this analysis providing the broader context for the period, the discussion will now shift to a more detailed examination of the interstate interaction between these states.

### Interstate interaction: cooperative reciprocity

As mentioned above, the interaction between Iran and Iraq evolved from the policy reversal punctuated by the Algiers Agreement, indicating the beginning of the second period of analysis. Beyond resolving the issues underlying the border conflict between the two countries, including control over the Shatt al Arab waterway, the agreement also stimulated moves towards the development of a Gulf security pact, led by Iran and Iraq. In April 1975, Saddam Hussein (cited in Hoagland, 1975: 16) initiated this dialogue by suggesting that one of the key provisions derived from within the Algiers Agreement was that "[t]he security of the Gulf is the responsibility of the Gulf states as a whole. This fact must come in the mainstream of talks which are to take place between Iran and the Gulf States, which include Iraq."

The following month the Shah concurred with this position, stating that "we both [Iran and Iraq] want to keep third parties out" (cited in Godsell, 1975: 3) of the Persian Gulf area. Saddam Hussein sustained the debate on the development of regional "security structures" (cited in Pace, 1975a: 2) to protect regional interests in the Gulf. It distinguished the post-Algiers atmosphere as a period conducive to 'regional détente' (Pace, 1975a). Indeed, the cooperative moves by both Iran and Iraq stimulated a shift within the foundations of Gulf security, indicating a shift from the aggressive articulation of Iranian desires for regional dominance, towards acquiescence by Iraqi towards cooperative participation with Iranian leadership (Morris, 1976).

Discussions into the possibility of developing a Gulf security pact continued in the following months, with renewed calls coming in June and July for the removal of foreign military bases within the Persian Gulf area by both the Shah and Saddam Hussein (Pace, 1975d: 3; Vicker, 1975). Hussein, in particular, was vocal in declaring Iraq's position that "we stand for declaring the Gulf as a peace zone cleared of all military bases of foreign countries, whatever their color and their size" (cited in Pace, 1975d: 3). June also saw the signing of a treaty between Iran and Iraq formally delineating their common border (*New York Times*, 1975b: 10).

By the end of 1975, Iran and Iraq had signed a succession of "good-neighbor agreements' that sought to regulate a range of border issues (*New York Times*, 1975c: 2). These included the interaction between Iranian and Iraqi border posts, navigation of the Shatt al Arab, and the movement of citizens between the two countries (*New York Times*, 1975c: 2). A period of relative calm had been instigated by the end of 1975, with the solidification of their relations post-Algiers, through the evolution of confidence-building measures. It also re-affirmed Iraq's territorial integrity, which remained a key policy priority for the Baathist party.

Despite the beginning of 1976 being marked by the recall of seven Iranian Ambassadors from neighboring states, including Iraq,[1] the relations between the two states remained peaceful throughout that year. The Shah maintained his position welcoming "any kind of firm or loose collective security pact, or even just an understanding" (cited in Cooley, 1976: 6) for the Gulf region. In addition, the Iranian National Assembly approved the introduction of an Iranian-Iraqi Friendship Treaty, which was to lay the foundations for further guidelines relating to border issues and peaceful interaction (Pace, 1976: 12).

In 1977, Iran–Iraq relations remained peaceful and cooperative, with both states faced by the problematic OPEC split on pricing which threatened to slash their oil profits (*The Times*, 1977). While Iran, Iraq, and the Persian Gulf states moved cooperatively to increase oil prices by 10 percent, Saudi Arabia sought to stabilize prices, resulting in a two-tier pricing system (*Chicago Tribune*, 1977: 4). With the higher oil prices demanded by the OPEC coalition led by Iran and Iraq, a direct consequence was a sharp decrease in their sales and profit, as demand shifted to cheaper petroleum products (*Chicago Tribune*, 1977: 4). These moves nevertheless were evidence of a renewed sense of cooperation between the two states, with the extension of collaboration to economic matters.

The year 1978 saw the continued drive by Tehran to establish a Persian Gulf security arrangement with Iraq and Saudi Arabia (Lewis, 1978). It was also reported to include considerations of Iraqi naval plans, which were to be strategically developed not to compete with either Saudi Arabia or Iran, yet enable a continued enhancement of Iraqi capabilities (Lewis, 1978). This agreement and the strategic limitations that were to be put on Iraqi military development demonstrate the subservient position that the Iraqis had been resigned to in their interstate interaction with Iran.

These moves were also part of a larger security dialogue that had been established between Iran and Iraq throughout this period, which also included other important Gulf states such as Saudi Arabia (Hijazlin, 1978). Empress Farah also extended a high-level visit to Iraq during 1978, the first in 25 years by a top member of the royal family (*New York Times*, 1978b: 21). The visit was considered as a sign of ongoing improvement in relations between the two countries, in spite of the backdrop of the Iranian revolution (*New York Times*, 1978b: 21).

The event that began the shift away from the détente of Iran–Iraq relations was the Iranian revolution. Beginning in 1978, the revolution took hold with growing unrest and political upheaval. January 1978 saw rioting after the government in Tehran had sought to discredit Ayatollah Khomeini, at the time a prominent Islamic leader based in Iraq.[2] Government troops had opened fire on protesters, in an attempt to disperse and discourage further public disruption. However, the move had the opposite effect (Thurgood, 1978: 6). Opposition to the government rapidly proliferated, first spreading to northwestern Iran and Tabriz in February, and then subsequently expanding to other provincial areas (IISS, 1978). Indeed, the growing stature of Ayatollah Khomeini in both the political and religious movement against the Shah and the building momentum of the Iranian revolution resulted in the Shah seeking his removal from Iraq. This occurred on October 3, 1978, with the acquiescence of the Iraqis, demonstrating the Iraqi willingness to support the Shah in resolving the domestic instability.

This, however, had no effect. By November 1978 the violence and civil unrest had spread across Iran and included strikes in the oil and public sector and violence in Tehran (Thurgood, 1978: 5). All the measures that were employed by the Shah failed to suppress the growing momentum of the movement against him, even including his formation of a military government (Branigin, 1978). The final effort by the Shah to maintain his grip on power was the abrupt move back towards civilian control headed by the anti-Shah, pro-nationalist leader Shahpour Bakhtiar (*Wall Street Journal*, 1979: 7).

The détente period 73

Bakhtiar began a series of wide ranging initiatives, including shifting the foreign policy of Iran away from regional hegemony to domestic solidification (Whitley and McDermott, 1979). The move proved unsuccessful and the Shah left Iran on 16 January 1979. Following the announcement that the armed forces would follow an official policy of neutrality, consequently brushing away the support that had been holding the interim government in power, Bakhtiar resigned (IISS, 1978). By February 1979, Ayatollah Khomeini triumphantly entered Iran, leading the revolution to its successful conclusion (IISS, 1979). This marked the end of the détente period and heralded a resultant shift in the relations between Iran and Iraq.

## Dynamic power distribution: rapid Iraqi power convergence

Like the Pre-Algiers period, the relations between the two states had conformed to the basic principle of reciprocity, that is, a "tit for tat" interaction. The détente period was characterized by cooperative calls between the two, with planning (albeit limited) of joint security pacts, and several treaties relating to their bilateral relations. Yet forming a backdrop to this cooperative interaction between Iran and Iraq throughout the period, the dynamic power capability distribution experienced a dramatic convergence resulting from revolutionary disorder in Iran. The Shah's social modernization and development programs empowered his opponents while simultaneously undermining his leadership, which had previously managed to keep these competing forces at bay. The Shah's demise was positively correlated with decreasing Iranian power. This can be clearly seen through a review of Iran's power position relative to Iraq during the détente period.

### *Demographic indicators: divergence and Iranian superiority*

Looking first at demographic indicators, we see that data relating to total population demonstrates that Iran was able to slightly extend its superiority over Iraq during the détente period. Tehran enjoyed a more consistent growth rate, with an average of 3.9 percent, compared with Iraq at 3.8 percent.[3] And although Iraq experienced the greatest annual growth rate, when in 1976–7 it grew by 4.56 percent,[4] Iran managed to extend its superiority slightly over the period.

74  *The détente period*

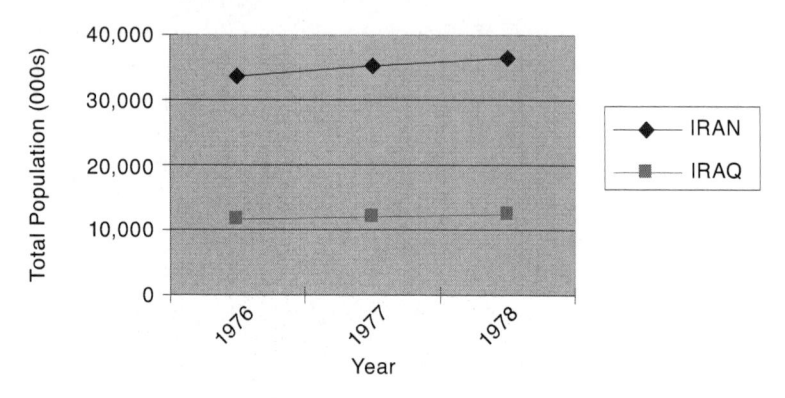

*Figure 4.1* Détente total population.

Iran also extended its superiority in urban population from 1975–8, on the back of significant growth in 1976–7, when the Iranian urban population grew by 16.9 percent.[5] This was by far the largest growth rate of the period, and far exceeding Iraq's best annual increase of 8 percent.[7] Consequently, Iran was able to extend its advantage from 1.8:1 in 1976 to 1.94:1 in 1978.

Yet while the initial analysis of demographic indicators suggest that Iran was able to extend its advantage it held over Iraq during the détente period, other indicators, including social stability, reveal a fundamentally different picture. In fact, on most indicators, Iraq dramatically narrowed the gap with Iran from 1975–8. The beginning of this convergence is evident in an analysis of economic capabilities.

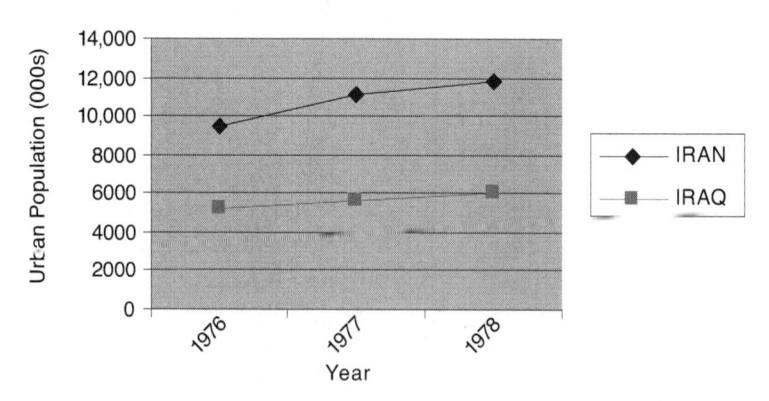

*Figure 4.2* Détente urban population.

## Economic capability: narrowing Iranian superiority

Although Iran was able to maintain a broad lead over Iraq with regard to GDP, Iraq began to narrow this gap throughout the détente period. This power convergence was due mainly to the overall downturn in Iranian GDP (–12 percent), matched by impressive Iraqi GDP growth (21.3 percent).[6] Even so, Iran was able to maintain the edge, with an advantage over Iraq of 3.5:1.[7]

The GDP per capita figures, meanwhile, show more starkly Iraq's economic convergence, with the Iranian superiority reduced to within parity parameters (under the 20 percent power threshold method of de Soysa et al., 1997).[8] This, as seen in GDP, was a result of an overall Iranian reduction (–18.5 percent), being matched by comparative growth in Iraq (12.5 percent).[9] It saw Iranian superiority reduce from 1.64:1 in 1976 to 1.18:1 in 1978.[10]

Economic capability indices therefore indicate that Iran was experiencing both a relative and comparative decline in its economic power. This is particularly evident in GDP per capita, during the détente period. It therefore suggests that although Iran was able to maintain its superiority (when considered in tandem with demographic indicators); Iraq was nevertheless able to reverse the initial divergence during 1970–5.

## Military power: Iraq's convergence on Iranian military power

A review of military power data shows that based on the first indicator, military expenditures, Iran was able to extend its position. Iraq was,

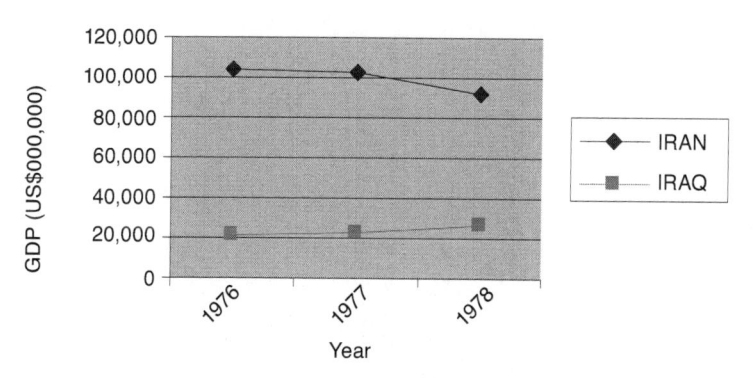

*Figure 4.3* Détente GDP.

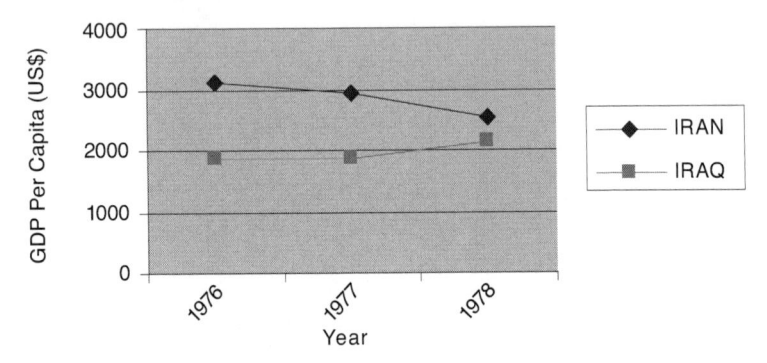

*Figure 4.4* Détente GDP.

however, able to experience a comparative convergence in 1977, with a growth of 14 percent, compared with Iran's growth of 2.9 percent.[11] However, in the following year the growth patterns were reversed, with Iran experiencing its highest growth (14.6 percent), and Iraq experiencing a decline (−1 percent).[12] Iran finished the détente period extending its considerable lead from 4.4:1 in 1976 to 4.6:1 in 1978.[13] This is demonstrated below.

Data relating to military personnel levels, however, suggests that Iraq attained convergence and parity with Iran during the détente Period. Initially, Iran maintained an advantage of 2.2:1 in 1976.[14] This was extended further in 1977, as Iran's advantage increased to 2.5:1. This occurred in spite of the fact that Iran's military personnel levels

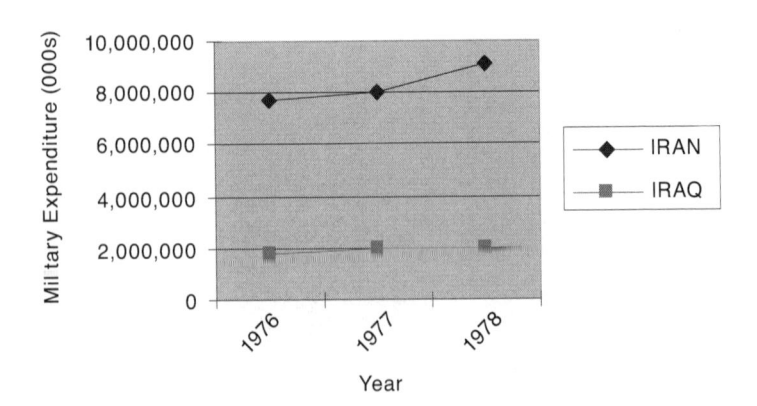

*Figure 4.5* Détente military expenditure.

decreased 16 percent in 1977 (to 350,000), and were subsequently maintained at that level in 1978.[15] The Iranian divergence in 1977 was largely as a result of a greater reduction in Iraqi personnel levels, with a 26 percent decrease from 190,000 to 140,000.[16] Nevertheless, in the following year Iraqi personnel levels reversed course, increasing by a massive 158 percent to 362,000,[17] leading to parity between both sides.

Military power indicators thus show that while Iran was able to slightly extend its advantage with regard to military expenditure, a decrease in overall military personnel (matched by an Iraqi increase) eroded this divergence. In fact, based on the convergence and transition that occurred in the military personnel indicator, the composite measure of military power indicators augmented the already declining Iranian power and suggests continuation of the convergence that was being experienced in relation to economic capabilities.

## *Military modernization and absorption: further Iraqi convergence on Iranian military power*

Military modernization and absorption proved to be a prominent factor in the power conversion of military expenditure throughout the détente period. Iran continued to accelerate the arms build-up it had embarked upon in the Pre-Algiers period. The instability created by the revolution at the end of the détente period, however, resulted in the evacuation of

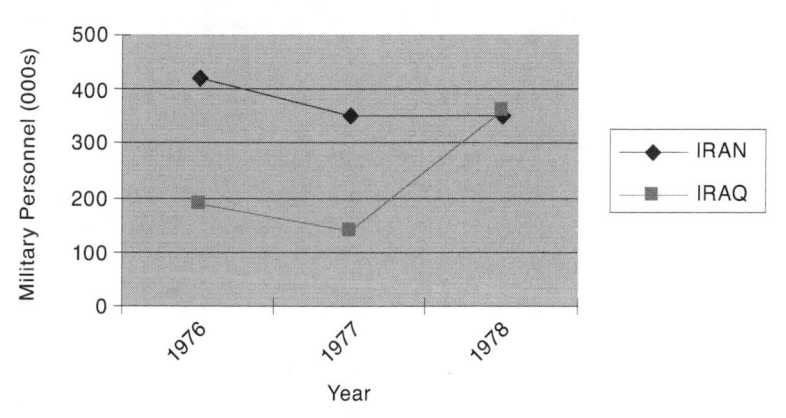

*Figure 4.6* Détente military personnel.

## 78  The détente period

large numbers of foreign personnel who had been critical in supporting the Iranian military modernization and integration of new foreign weapon systems (IISS 1976: 24). The difficulty faced by the Iranian military in integrating this material becomes abundantly clear if one looks at the sources of their military equipment and agreements for the supply of equipment throughout the 1970s.

Beginning in 1971, Iran concluded an agreement with Britain to supply the first installment of Chieftain Tanks, with some 800 agreed upon. Iran also undertook an extensive agreement with the US to augment its airlift capabilities with the agreement to supply 30 C-130H aircraft (IISSb, 1972/73). The following year major contracts were again signed between the US, Britain and Iran—with the US agreeing to supply F-5E fighter aircraft and TOW missiles, while Britain agreed to supply Seacat SAM and hovercraft for naval patrol (IISSd, 1973/74). Late 1972 also saw a rapid expansion of agreements between Iran and the US. Equipment ranged from F-5E (111) to P-3C Orions (6), Bell 214A utility (287) and Bell AH-1J armed (202) Helicopters, F-4 Phantoms (70), and Boeing 707-320 transport/tanker aircraft (6) (IISSd, 1973/74). More agreements also emerged with Britain for Scorpion light tanks, and Italy for AB-205A helicopters (46) (IISSe, 1974/45). Early in 1974 Iran signed its largest single contract up to that date, with the purchase of the F-14 fighter (80), with a smaller purchase from Italy (22 Chinook helicopters), France (Combattante), and Britain (Blindfire radar) (IISSe, 1974/75).

In late 1974 and early 1975 the rapid proliferation trend continued with the US agreeing to supply Spruance-class destroyers (6), Tang-Class submarines (3), F-4E fighter (36), KC 135 tankers (6), and a communications intelligence system (IISSg, 1976/77). In 1975 Iran also signed an additional contract with Britain for 1,200 more Chieftain Tanks (IISSg, 1976/77). Late 1975 and early 1976 saw the continued expansive military acquisition program by Iran with smaller purchases from Britain (radars, scout cars, landing craft, SAM), France, the Netherlands, and the US (helicopter, transport/tanker aircraft, and TOW) (IISSh, 1977/78). Throughout late 1976 and early 1977 Iran continued acquiring its armaments from Britain (Rapier SAM on tracked vehicles and Scorpion light tanks), Italy (2 AS-61 helicopter), the US (Sidewinder, Phoenix, and Sparrow AAM; 160 F-16 fighters, Hawk SAM, P-3C Orions, 50 CH-47 Chinooks, and Bell 214A helicopters). It also saw the first foray by the Iranians into obtaining supplies from the USSR (SAM, ATK guns, ZSU-23-4 AA guns, and BMP mechanized infantry combat vehicles) (IISSh, 1977/78). The year 1978 witnessed the last large orders under the Shah with equipment sourced from the US (E-3 AWACS and F-4E), Italy (Lupo-class frigates), Germany (type 209 subs), and Britain (support vessels) (IISSi, 1978/79).

Its forces were flooded by foreign equipment all requiring integration and foreign support to do this. The military modernization program undertaken under the Shah had required these foreign personnel for maintenance, training and integration of new equipment into its forces, with some estimates suggesting the need for at least 50–60,000 foreign specialists (IISS, 1976). The support that had been keeping the Iranian military forces functioning rapidly began to unravel at the end of the détente period, severely impacting on their ability to translate their military expenditures into tangible power capabilities.

Iraq, on the other hand, maintained a phased integration of new equipment into its armed forces, again paying particular attention to the air force and army. Looking first at the Iraqi air force, the beginning of this period saw the Iraqis introduce the front-line Soviet fighter of the time, the MiG 23, in addition to continuing the phased introduction of the MiG 21 (IISSf, 1975/76). Continued expansion occurred through 1977 and 1978, with the number of MiG-23B (90) and MiG-21 (115) aircraft continuing to expand the Iraq combat aircraft out to 369 and approximately 25,000 personnel (IISSi, 1978/79). The Iraqi air force also continued to expand its force multipliers with seven helicopter squadrons providing increased ground support for the army (IISSi, 1978/79).

A similar process of gradually increasing equipment was evident in the Iraqi army. In 1976 Iraq made the initial introduction of the T-62 tank, accompanied by the cycled decrease of purchases for the older T-55/54 (IISSf, 1975/76). This process continued through 1977 into 1978, with a slight increase in overall number of tanks, from 1,200 to 1,350 (IISSg, 1976/77; IISSh, 1977/78). The Iraqi army was also aided by simplicity of use of the new hardware. Iraqi armored capability developed from the basic T-55/54 tank which had emerged in the late 1940s, towards the T-62 which was a positive development for its overall ground capabilities. Although the Iranian Chieftain provided for a highly advanced front line tank relative to the Iraqi T-62, Iraq was able to better integrate these tanks into field service. In addition, the Iraqis sought to augment their land forces with Scud missiles (IISSf, 1975/76). This reflected the concentrated effort by Iraq to effectively integrate new equipment into its forces.[18]

The period also witnessed the Iraqis continuing willingness to source equipment from other countries, started in 1974 with the signing of an agreement with France for 40 Alouette Helicopter (IISSf, 1975/76). In 1976 the Iraqi government again signed an agreement for the purchase of more helicopters from France (10 Super Frelon) (IISSh, 1977/78). It ended the period seeking to augment its Air Force capabilities with the purchase of 36 Mirage F1 fighters and four trainers (IISSi, 1978/79) from France.

Military advisors, particularly from the Soviet Union, also helped train Iraqis extensively in new weapons systems, allowing them to absorb their new capabilities effectively (Karsh, 1987/88). So although its program was expansive, it was aimed towards developing existing capabilities with the phased introduction of more advanced equipment matching the Iraqis' ability to integrate these into its services.

Consequently, despite spending an amount 4.6 times greater than Iraq on military expenditure by 1978, Iran's ability to convert its military material acquisition into capabilities was severely undermined. The speed of its acquisition strategy, in addition to the exodus of foreign personnel supporting its integration, served to negate the Iranian military power superiority. Conversely, Iraq's directed and moderated military modernization program, supported by the USSR, allowed the effective translation of its military material resources into power capabilities. Iraq was thus able to continue its process of convergence on Iranian superiority.

*Social stability: growing parity*

Factors relating to social stability further augmented the process of Iraqi convergence seen in the other power indicators throughout the détente period. Iran's modernization and industrialization program was a key element in this convergence, paradoxically undermining Iran's overall power capabilities. It weakened the Shah, and led eventually to the revolution at the end of the period.

The development and modernization process that was undertaken by the Shah sought to stimulate economic opportunities for the Iranian population (Seale, 1978). It created increasing demands, particularly from urban areas, for a greater share in the distribution of jobs and money within the economy.[19] This growth also stimulated a shift in the distribution of the population, with a massive increase in rural-to-urban population migration, which served to accentuate the demands that were being placed on the imperial regime (Pace, 1975c; Randal, 1978: 22; Tuohy, 1975; Vakil, 1976). One such example of this massive population shift can be seen in the span of ten years, 1963–73; the population of Tehran boomed from some 300,000 residents to over four million. The process of which strained the infrastructure to breaking point, with outlying farms transformed with huge apartment and office buildings, and city hotels booked three years in advance (Hopkirk, 1975: 6). A practical consequence of this shift was a massive burgeoning of the urban mass demanding a share in the new jobs within the economy (IISS, 1978).

It was within this migrating mass that social dislocations accelerated and exacerbated the growing depth of discontent with the Shah (IISS, 1978). This was particularly the case with young Iranian men from rural, outlying areas who moved to the urban population centers in search of higher-paid employment (IISS, 1978). Put simply, this was because demand for new employment outstripped supply. The Iranian government, unable to deal with rapid changes in rural-urban distribution, could not avoid large-scale unemployment. Rural migrants struggled to subsist in shanty towns in the outlying areas of cities while they waited for employment opportunities. This inevitably led to friction and created a solid base for the revolution, especially amongst unemployed rural migrants bordering major cities (Moran, 1978/79).

This, in tandem with the Shah's process of unwinding his "tightly muzzled power system" (Seale, 1978: 4), actually had the effect of assisting opposition groups to act against the Shah, resulting in widespread protests and riots. Various groups made increasing demands upon the imperial regime, including the expressed desire for more freedom and fundamental change from what was seen as an autocratic, decadent and corrupt regime.[20] These groups ranged from all different backgrounds, and sought to articulate their opposition to the Shah. Liz Thurgood (September 26, 1978: 5) highlights this in her article "Tehran Paradox – Security Crackdown for Freedom," suggesting that the opposition to the Shah cuts across all sectors of the society, embracing Westernized intellectuals, religious bazaari's, unhappy housewives, and lower-middle-class students. Whoever raises a banner against the Government (and by implication the Shah)—whether Communist, Right-wing nationalist, or a Mullah—is virtually guaranteed an instant following.

Indeed, this is also noted by Colin Smith (in Branigin, 1978: 8), suggesting that the opposition to the Shah was made up of "very disparate people," who were only united by a driving hatred for the Shah's rule.

This helped create an opportunity for opposition groups to effectively utilize modern communication tools (including newspapers and propaganda papers) to tap into this growing discontent, with the literacy programs enabling a wider cross-section of the community to be reached (IISS, 1978). A particularly pertinent example occurred following the initial riots in Qom during the start of 1978, when leading religious leaders, including Ayatollah Shariat-Madari,[21] began issuing pamphlets openly criticizing the government. These were widely circulated throughout the country, and condemned the government for its actions in attempting to quell the riots. In a letter published by Ayatollah Shariat-Madari the government response was labeled "un-Islamic and inhumane," with calls made for those taking part in the suppression to be punished (Thurgood, 1978: 6).

To condemn the government was an unprecedented step by these religious leaders. The regime attempted to challenge them through the widespread censorship of newspaper publications. Once widespread dissatisfaction spread, however, it was unable to be restrained through the use of censorship, and was further stimulated through the Shah's ever-increasing liberalization programs.[22] Even the Shah's attempts to diffuse the social tension with "carrot and stick" neo-liberalist policies, including the installation of a civilian government (Branigin 1978: 8; Seale, 1978: 4; Thurgood, 1978: 5), failed to halt the inevitable revolution at the end of 1978.[23]

Iraq, on the other hand, had overcome the destabilizing Kurdish guerrilla movement in the Pre-Algiers period to enter into a period of relative domestic calm. This had absorbed Iraqi military operations until a resolution was reached in 1975, with the effective collapse of guerrilla forces, following the removal of Iran's military backing. Arguably the most important support the Kurds had received came from the Iranian military was artillery, which had enabled the Kurds to counter the heavy mechanized and armored Iraqi military. Following the conclusion of the 1975 Algiers Agreement, Iranian support, and its artillery, was removed, leading to the collapse of the Kurdish movement (Roberts, 1975: 6; Young, 1975: 9). Enhanced social stability following the suppression of the Kurdish movement enabled the Iraqi armed forces to concentrate on its expansion and modernization and in turn strengthened the central authority of the Baathist regime (*Daily Star*, 1975h: 2).

The Baathist regime did, nevertheless, continue to face more limited opposition from other domestic sources, and most importantly from the Iraqi Communist Party (ICP). After seizing power in 1968, the Iraqi regime undertook a crackdown on the ICP, hanging a number of leading party members (Cooley, 1971: 14). At the beginning of the 1970s, however, the Baathist regime had seen it necessary to reconcile its history of violence with the ICP, in order to reach agreement with the USSR on the important Soviet–Iraqi friendship treaty.[24] The ICP was brought into the Iraqi cabinet,[25] and joined a joint 'Progressive National Front' with the Baathist regime (*New York Times*, 1978a: 3).

The Communist party was largely tolerated until reports emerged from the Iraqi Communist Central Committee in 1978 criticizing the Baathist regime. These reports demanded greater equality in power sharing between the Baathist government and ICP, and went so far as to criticize the increase in economic cooperation between Iraq and the West (Howe, 1979: 2). Following these reports the Baathist regime undertook a series of purges, imprisoning and executing up to 1,000 Iraqi Communists (Cooley, 1978: 4). This included the arrest of eight members of the Iraqi Communist Central Committee who had released the anti-government statements (*New York Times*, 1978a: 3). During this period the Baathist regime was therefore able to effectively shift its policy from conciliation to suppression (Howe, 1979: 2).

Iraq was also able to continue on its process of modernization with its widespread labor-force skill-enhancement program, including free education and mandatory literacy campaigns (Cockburn, 1977: 6; *Daily Star*, 1971a: 3; Broder, 1979: 11). Despite the benefits associated with these reforms, Iraq still faced an underlying challenge in the development of its economy—a shortage of skilled labor (Cockburn, 1977: 6). Education policies were enacted which enabled further manipulation of the emerging employment opportunities into beneficial sectors (*Daily Star*, 1971a: 3). In 1977 alone, government investment in education increased by a staggering 84 percent (Cockburn, 1977: 6). This was matched by the desire of the Baathist regime to improve the quality of its manpower (Cockburn, 1977: 6).

For Iraq, the détente period was therefore one that was characterized by a further solidification of Baathist authority, with the piece-by-piece removal of domestic threats. Iraq was also able to continue re-structuring the education sector and economy, with an accelerated investment cycle to address some underlying weaknesses in productive inputs. This suggests that, when taken in conjunction with other power capability indicators, social stability was instrumental in Iraq's convergence towards power parity with Iran.

## Moderately salient issues and a cooperative cycle: a peaceful conclusion

The tone of the détente period was clearly established through the Algiers Agreement, resolving the issues that had stimulated conflictual foreign policy interaction in the preceding period. The posturing by Iraq in attempting to counter Iranian influence and regional projection vanished, to be replaced by cooperative calls to collaborate in providing security for the Gulf region. At the same time, the Baathist party was able to re-establish firm societal control, particularly over the Kurdish regions which had been a pronounced threat to the territorial integrity of Iraq. The ability to quell this threat was largely attributable to the removal of Iranian military support.

Iran and Iraq therefore began the period exhibiting very cooperative foreign policy interactions, although when considered with the insights offered by examining interstate interaction and foreign policy reciprocity, we can see that the initial attempts at formulating peaceful relations between the two countries were extensively undertaken during the Iranian preponderance experienced at the beginning of the period. The relationship continued to be largely cooperative, however, particularly regarding continued initiatives towards a potential security agreement between Iran and Iraq. The year 1977 also showed that these cooperative relations between Iran and Iraq were not limited to border or security arrangements, with joint moves to increase oil prices at OPEC.

Perhaps one of the most significant signs of the positive and cooperative relationship that had been established between the two countries was the expulsion of Ayatollah Khomeini, who had been further inciting the revolutionary forces against the Shah. This came at a time when the dynamic comparative power relations between the two countries were at their greatest convergence, with a rapid move towards parity by the Iraqis. And in spite of this opportunity to capitalize on the domestic instability in Iran, Iraq maintained their cooperative stance. This is interesting as it suggests that the issue resolution that occurred as a result of the Algiers Agreement, enabling Iran to project its regional dominance and Iraq to secure its domestic control, did indeed have a positive and lasting effect on the relations between the two countries, removing the basis from which these states had been fighting. Iraq did not seek to capitalize on the domestic instability of Iran, and re-secure their historical territorial claims that had been seceded with the Algiers Agreement.

The two periods thus far suggest the importance of issues in stimulating the conflict, and power capabilities in restricting the escalation of conflict to war. Examining the interstate interaction and foreign policy reciprocity between these states has also allowed the delineation of clear patterns of interaction, with both conflict and cooperative cycles. The question now emerges as to whether in the lead up to the Iran–Iraq War there were: (i) highly salient issues under contention; (ii) a reciprocal and conflictual cycle of interstate interaction; or (iii) permissive conditions for escalation to war, with a power transition between Iran and Iraq.

# 5 The post-revolution period

Phase 3 of Iran–Iraq relations

This chapter explores the final phase of Iran–Iraq relations, beginning with the institution of the revolutionary government in 1979 and ending in the escalation of conflict to war in 1980. This chapter will demonstrate the dramatic shift that occurred in these state's relations with the elevation of Ayatollah Khomeini as supreme leader, with the emergence of two highly salient issues—the Iranian desire for Pan-Shi'ism in the region, and Iraq concerns for state integrity and survival. The resolution of these issues will be illustrated through examining their foreign policy reciprocity, demonstrating a highly reciprocal and conflictual evolution of relations to the point of war in September 1980. An examination of dynamic power capabilities will then be utilized to highlight the permissive conditions for the continued evolution of their conflictual interactions to war, removing the major constraints that had been evident in earlier periods preventing full-blown fighting.

**Issues under contention: Pan-Shi'ism, state integrity, and survival**

As noted above, the installation of the revolutionary government in Iran marked the beginning of a dramatic shift in the relations between Iran and Iraq. Although the ruling Baathist party in Iraq greeted the new revolutionary government in Iran with a welcoming and cooperative posture, these moves were not reciprocated. Indeed, the Iranians began to implement a number of policies to reflect the preferences of the new supreme leader, Ayatollah Khomeini. This was to set the tone of their interactions, and resulted in the emergence of two key issues from which these states contended—Iranian regional aspirations towards Pan-Shi'ism and Iraq concerns for state integrity and survival.

Looking first at Iran, although continuing the Shah's ambition in projecting Iranian power within the region, the revolutionary government had other motivations in doing so. Most clearly enunciated by a leading aide to Khomeini, Ayatollah Montazeri, Iran sought to export their "Islamic revolution to all the Muslim countries of the world" (cited in the *Chicago Tribune*, 1979: 22). The new government challenged the legitimacy of neighboring countries, with suggestions from high ranking officials—including the then Iranian President—that states in the region were not independent, with external direction from major powers including the US. The articulation of this issue by the Iranians demonstrated highly salient tangible and intangible values.

The ascendancy of the Islamic forces within the revolutionary change of Iranian government resulted in intangible religious values being of utmost importance. This was embodied in the articulated Iranian drive towards exporting their Islamic revolution to neighboring countries, as well as the broader aim of supporting a Pan-Shi'ism movement. The manifestation of this movement had distinct tangible values as well, with the propagation of instability in neighboring countries brought about by Islamic emissaries from Iran encouraging protest and revolution. This also opened opportunities to extend Iranian territorial resources and wealth.

The second key issue under contention throughout the period was Iraqi security and survival. Iranian moves towards exporting their revolution witnessed the emergence of another fundamental threat to the Baathist ability to maintain internal control. With some 60 percent of their population constituting Shi'ite Muslims, the potential for a Pan-Shi'ism movement to destabilize the entire security of the Iraqi state was a visible and pressing threat. Having experienced the undermining effect of the Kurdish separatist movement, this would have reinforced the highly salient nature of the threat.

Moreover, given the nature of the political identity rooted in secular Arab socialism, the Islamic nature of this movement also threatened not only their independent functioning but also the Iraqi political identity, with the real possibility of division and control by a supranational Islamic movement stemming from Iran. The Iranian revolutionary government, for its part, reinforced the threat that must have been felt by the

Baathist government, with even Khomeini himself openly encouraging the Iraqi population to overthrow the Iraqi government.

Thus, interstate interaction throughout the period evolved against the backdrop of the active Iranian policy for Pan-Shi'ism and the renewed Iraqi desire to secure their central authority and survival as an independent functioning state.

## Interstate interaction: escalatory and reciprocal conflict spiral

In the lead-up to war, this phase of Iranian and Iraqi interaction was characterized by a shift experienced with the installation of the Iranian revolutionary government. As noted above, this government instituted numerous policy shifts, reflecting Ayatollah Khomeini's preferences for Pan-Shi'ism and Pan-Islamism (IISS, 1979). Despite these changes, Iraq initially greeted the change of government in the spirit of cooperation. The Iraqi minister for information, Saad Qasim Hammudi (cited in Howe, 1979: 11), enunciated this stance, stating that "we are not concerned about any change in Iran so long as it doesn't affect the people of Iraq" and that Iraq desired "the closest relations of fruitful cooperation" with Iran. Iran was, nonetheless, viewed by Iraq with great caution following the revolution (Howe, 1979: 11). Iraq's significant population of Shi'ite Muslims, recent cooperative relations with the Shah, and the expulsion of Ayatollah Khomeini from his exile in Najaf all sought to exacerbate this posture (Howe, 1979: 11; Lippman, 1979: 20).

Iraq had good reason to be concerned. Although stringently denying any intention to export revolution to neighboring countries, Iranian officials clearly engaged in revolutionary rhetoric with the hope it would spread (IISS, 1979: 47).[1] In fact, Iran began using Islamic emissaries, acting on behalf of its religious leadership and acting independently of its official embassies (*Chicago Tribune*, 1979: 22). These emissaries acted as mouthpieces for the Iranian government, calling for uprisings and inciting Shi'ite minorities in neighboring countries (or in some cases majorities, such as in Iraq and Bahrain). According to Ayatollah Montazeri, a leading aide of Ayatollah Khomeini, emissaries were an attempt to "export our Islamic revolution to all the Muslim countries of the world" (cited in the *Chicago Tribune*, 1979: 22). In Iraq, Iranian emissaries were blamed for a series of demonstrations against the

Baathist regime throughout 1979 (*Chicago Tribune*, 1979: 22; Ibrahim, 1979: 9; Kifner, 1979: 3).

By June accusations were emerging from the Iraqi government that Iran was actively supporting the Iraqi Shi'ite movement (Branigin, 1979: 18). Iran reciprocated, accusing the Iraqi government of shooting at anti-government protestors in Najaf, following the house arrest of a leading Shi'ite leader (Branigin, 1979: 18). Shortly thereafter, Iran began making accusations of Iraqi attacks in the border areas, while simultaneously renewing its claim on Bahrain (Branigin, 1979: 18; *Chicago Tribune*, 1979: 8; Lamr, 1979).

A few months later Iraq had renounced its obligations under the Algiers Agreement, with the Iraqi ambassador to Iran, Abdul Hussein Hassan, calling for revolutionary government to allow Arab, Baluchi, and Kurdish minorities self-rule (Randal, 1979: 29). Hassan also called for Iran to remove its forces from the three islands in the Strait of Hormuz that it had occupied in 1971 (Randal, 1979: 29). Iran matched the Iraqi moves, with its own calls for the Shi'ite majority in the south,[2] and the Kurdish minority in the north of Iraq to overthrow the Baathist government.

Events quickly escalated at the beginning of 1980. By March the Iranian ambassador to Iraq, Mohammed Duaei, had been expelled on charges of providing "false information" about Iraq (*New York Times*, 1980a: 9). The Iranian president, Abolhassan Bani-Sadr, launched a verbal attack on the Gulf states, suggesting that they were "not fully independent and are subservient to the United States" (cited in the *New York Times*, 1980b: 12). Moreover, he explicated Iranian policy for the Persian Gulf, suggesting Iran "was not interested in good relations with the Arab nations on the Persian Gulf" (cited in the *New York Times*, 1980b: 12).

In April 1980, an assassination attempt was made on Tariq Aziz, the Iraqi deputy prime minister (Branigin, 1980: 1), by Iranian revolutionaries (Karsh, 1987–8; McManus, 1980: 10; Temko, 1980: 6). Iraq accused Iran of complicity in the attack, and subsequently withdrew its entire embassy staff from Tehran (Temko, 1980: 6). Initial reports also began to emerge on border incidents between Iran and Iraq.[3] These included an Iranian accusation that Iraqi forces had attacked its oil facilities (*Los Angeles Times*, 1980a: 14), to air battles between the two states involving helicopters and fighter jets (*Los Angeles Times*, 1980b: 1;

*Los Angeles Times*, 1980c: 10). Iraq, led by President Saddam Hussein, also revived attempts to establish a Persian Gulf defense pact to protect against Iranian expansionism, reiterating the 'illegitimate' nature of Iran's occupation of the three islands within the Strait of Hormuz (Kifner, 1980c: 3).

During this period Iraq was again accused of expelling up to 40,000 Iranians from Iraq.[4] Iraq made representations to the United Nations that its actions were solely in response to the acts of terrorism committed against innocent Iraqi civilians, and the undeniable threat that they posed to the internal security of Iraq.[5] Ayatollah Khomeini responded by urging the Iraqi people to "wake up and topple this corrupt regime in your Islamic country before it's too late" (cited in the *New York Times*, 1980c: 14).[6] Hussein retorted, "[A]nyone that tries to put his hand on Iraq will have his hand cut off without hesitation. Iraq is prepared to enter into any kind of battle to defend its honor and sovereignty" (cited in the *New York Times*, 1980c: 14).

Sporadic violent conflict on the border occurred throughout the period until September,[7] by which time both Iran and Iraq were reporting almost daily clashes and ongoing diplomatic protests.[8] Both sides increasingly mobilized their armed forces to counter the increased threat. On September 17, 1980, Iraq again announced to the world that it had terminated the Algiers Agreement (*Los Angeles Times*, 1980g: 1; *New York Times*, 1980d: 8). By the night of 22 September, major hostilities had begun in the Iran–Iraq War, when Iraqi jets crossed into Iranian territory and struck Iranian Air Force targets on the ground.[9]

The post-revolution period continued to demonstrate that bilateral interaction between Iran and Iraq was characterized by reciprocity. A "tit for tat" scenario emerged following the early news of the takeover by the revolutionary government in 1979, with Iranian calls for revolution initially met with the Iraqi expulsion of Iranian citizens residing within its borders. Relations quickly deteriorated, with both Iran and Iraq attempting to create instability in their opponent's population. Border skirmishes and pitched battles between their military forces eventually evolved from the hostile relations in 1979, escalating to full-scale war in September 1980.

While this examination of the issues under contention and interstate interaction has demonstrated what these states are fighting about, and how the evolution of their relations reached the point of war in 1980, it does not in itself allow the differentiation from the first cycle which equally experienced highly salient issues in a reciprocal conflict cycle. I argue that the dynamic power capabilities that were evident in this period created permissive conditions for Iraq in escalating their conflict to war. This therefore differentiates and distinguishes the nature of relations between Iran and Iraq, and enables the more thorough explanation of why these states went to war when they did.

## Dynamic power distribution: Iraqi power convergence and transition

Examining this more closely, we see that this conflict escalated to war as the comparative power position of Iran and Iraq experienced further convergence and transition during the escalation of conflict. The constraining force of Iranian power preponderance (as seen in the Pre-Algiers period) had been removed, and the parity and transition that characterized their relations allowed Iraq to continue to escalate to war.

### *Demographic indicators: continued Iranian superiority*

Looking first at demographic indicators, we see that total population remains fairly stable with Iran slightly extending its superiority for the post-revolution period. Iran's growth for the period was 3.90 percent (while Iraq experienced growth of 3.25 percent).[10] The Iranian lead thus grew from 2.94:1 in 1979 to 2.96:1 in 1980.[11]

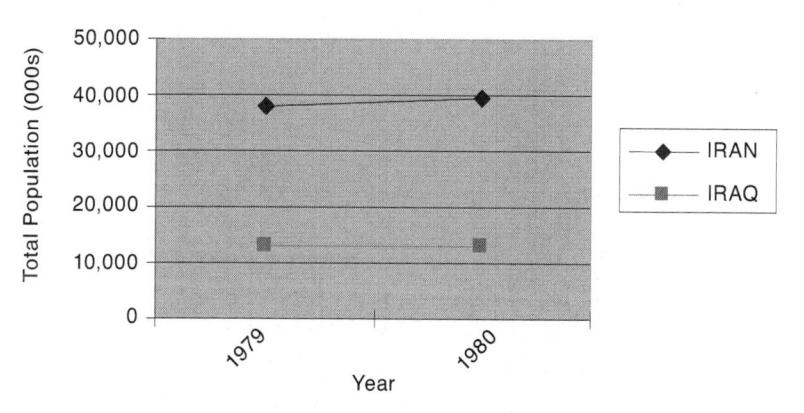

*Figure 5.1* Post-revolution total population.

92  *The post-revolution period*

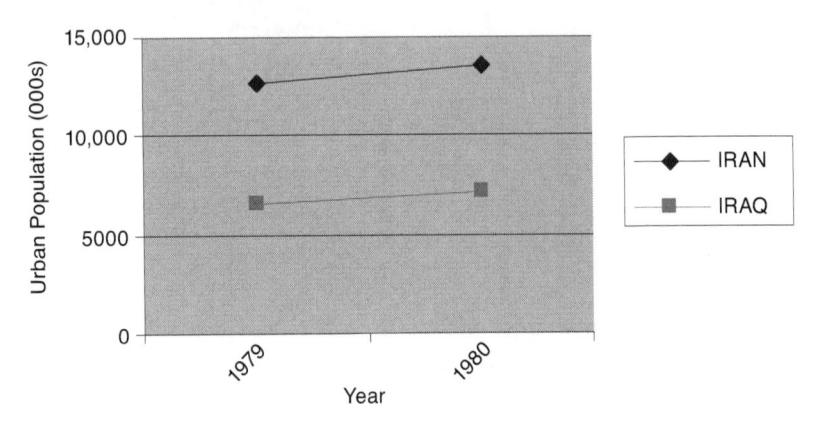

*Figure 5.2* Post-revolution urban population.

Urban population data, however, tells a different story, in which Iraq converged on Iran's superiority. Iraqi urban growth for the period was 8 percent, (compared with Iran, where growth was 7 percent).[12] The Iraqi convergence narrowed the Iranian advantage from 1.92:1 in 1979 to 1.90:1 in 1980.[13]

While demographic indicators suggest that Iran was able to maintain its broad lead over Iraq, this only reveals part of the power picture in the post-revolution period. By far the most important changes were evident in comparative economic and military indicators.

## *Economic capability: Iraqi convergence on Iranian superiority*

Indeed, while GDP data shows Iran was able to maintain its superiority, it did so despite some Iraqi convergence. Examining more closely, it is evident that Iraq was able to experience this convergence on the back of a smaller decline (−2.85 percent) in relative GDP to Iran (−12.8 percent).[14]

GDP Per Capita figures, on the other hand, suggest that the Iraqi position had moved from parity to superiority during the post-revolution period. Iraqi GDP Per Capita diverged from Iran throughout the period, even though it experienced a 6 percent decrease overall.[15] This was primarily attributable to a greater decrease by Iran for the period (at −15 percent).[16] Consequently, Iraq was able to extend its advantage

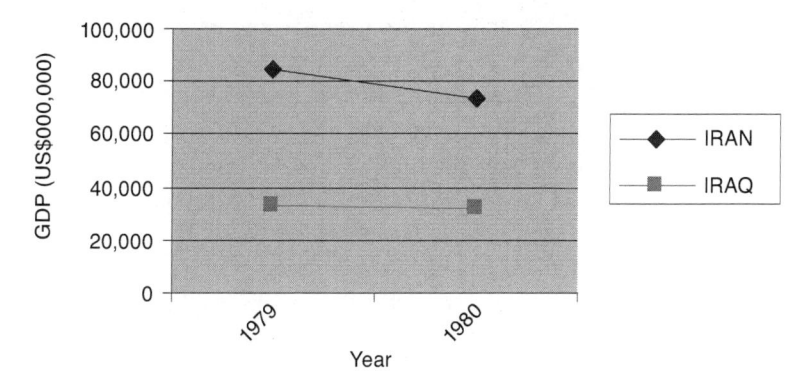

*Figure 5.3* Post-revolution GDP.

from 1.18:1 at the beginning of the period to finish with an overall superiority of 1.31:1 over Iran.[17]

The Iraqi divergence and superiority seen in GDP Per Capita thus augmented its process of convergence in overall GDP. It suggests that when economic capability is considered with the analysis of demographic indicators, Iraq was able to experience a convergence on Iranian superiority.

## *Military power: power transition*

An assessment of military indices further demonstrates the extent of the power convergence. Iran began the post-revolution period with overall

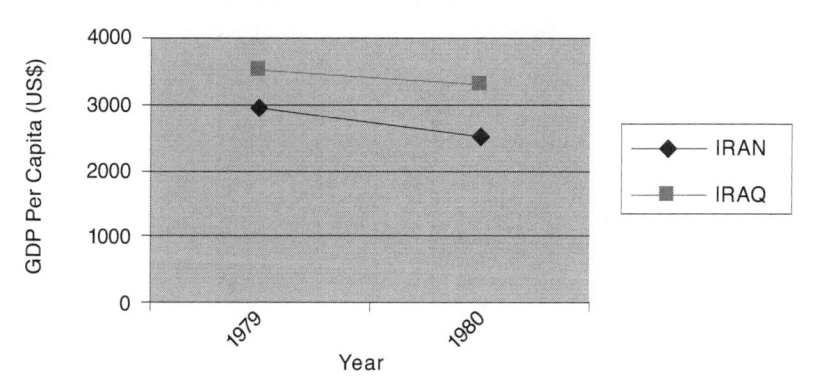

*Figure 5.4* Post-revolution GDP per capita.

94  *The post-revolution period*

superiority, with military spending at over 2:1 compared with Iraq.[18] However, the Iranian decrease of 38 percent for the period, matched by an Iraqi increase of 26.5 percent, resulted in a rapid convergence and parity in comparative military expenditure.[19]

Comparative military personnel figures further highlight this trend. Iraq began the period having experienced a 22.65 percent increase; however, this was muted somewhat by the decrease of 3.15 percent during 1978–80.[20] While Iran began the period with an increase of 18.57 percent, by 1980 its military personnel had decreased by

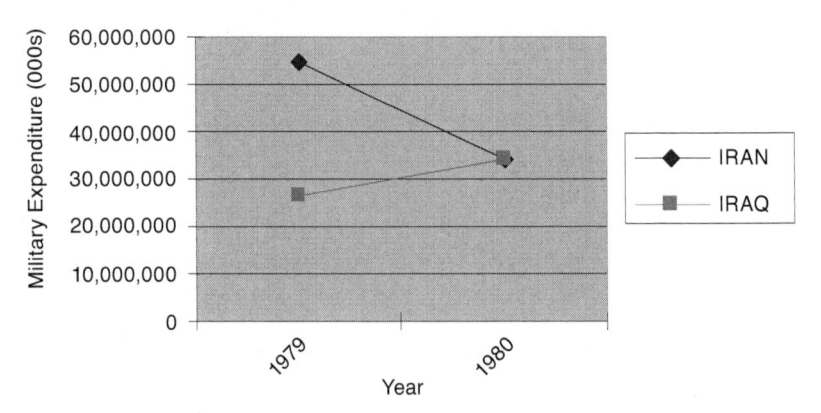

*Figure 5.5* Post-revolution military expenditure.

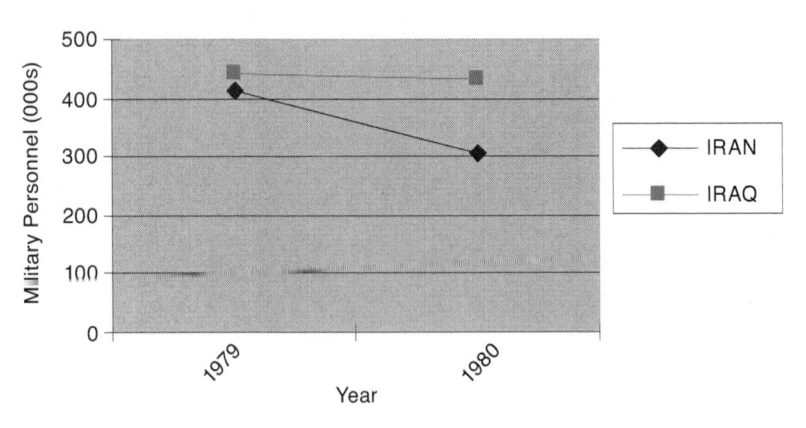

*Figure 5.6* Post-revolution military personnel.

26.51 percent.[21] The greater rate of decrease experienced by Iran thus accentuated Iraqi superiority, and Baghdad closed the period with a 1.4:1 advantage.

Both military power indicators therefore show that Iraq was able to not only achieve parity with Iran, but also experience a power transition. Taken in conjunction with economic capability and demographic indicators, Iraq had clearly enhanced its power relative to Iran. This, however, does not complete the power picture for Iran and Iraq. Indeed, the two power conversion factors—military modernization and absorption, and social stability—remain critical in delivering an accurate view of Iranian and Iraqi power.

### *Military modernization and absorption: increasing parity*

The military modernization program and absorption capacity of Iran and Iraq reached a critical juncture during the post-revolution period. Iranian military expansionism, although effectively halted in 1979 by the removal of the Shah (Whitley and McDermott, 1979) and the installation of the revolutionary government, did enjoy residual growth from orders carried over prior to the revolution. The Iranian Air Force, for example, increased its number of aircraft from 341 in 1978 to 459 in 1979 (IISSh, 1978/79; IISSi, 1979/80). Likewise, the army finished the period with 875 Chieftain Tanks in its inventory, up from 760 in 1978 (IISSh, 1978/79; IISSi, 1979/80).

However, this accentuated the absorption problems that were already evident, and further exacerbated the inability of the Iranian armed force to make use of their new acquisitions once war was imminent. As already noted, the flight of foreign trainers in 1978 and 1979 made this even more problematic. The final straw came when the US completely withdrew its support after the embassy hostage siege in Tehran, with the complete removal of American support in training, equipping, resupplying, and maintaining the Iranian military machine.[22] Thus, the rapid proliferation of highly advanced military equipment, recruitment issues, removal of US aid, and the significant decreases in Iranian military expenditures from 1979, all served to undermine the military capabilities of Iran.

Iraq, on the other hand, continued its more incremental approach, gradually introducing new military equipment, within both the army and air force, in the form of the T-62 tank and MiG-23 fighter.[23] Although Iraqi hardware lacked the sophistication of platforms within the Iranian armed forces, it was nonetheless more effective, based largely on its simplicity. Its ease of use and ability to be readily integrated into existing Iraqi forces allowed for actualized capability development and expansion (Hijazi, 1977: 7; IISS, 1973; IISS, 1974; IISS, 1975; Kutschera, 1971: 3; *Observer*, 1973: 6).

As a result the initial convergence and transition evident in raw military power was also evident in these findings, suggesting that Iraq not only experienced a military power transition, but in fact was also able to gain military superiority over Iran by 1980.

## Social stability: power transition

The final power conversion factor, social stability, takes the findings of this research in relation to Iranian and Iraqi comparative power positions one step further. It suggests that Iraq was actually able to experience an overall power transition with Iran, due to the widespread social instability that had plagued Iran for the period.

Following the revolution, marked by the return of Ayatollah Khomeini and the installation of a revolutionary provisional government, social stability did not return to Iran. Rather, Khomeini—along with the provisional government—instituted a series of purges resulting in many of the top officials and formally loyal personnel imprisoned or executed (Ramazani, 1980). Many of those most closely associated to the Shah had been in the officer corps (Branigin, 1978: 8), and this sector was purged especially heavily (Davison, 1979). All military sponsorship, arrangements, and previously generous treatment under the Shah were also immediately withdrawn (*Observer*, 1979: 8). The military's surrender to the revolutionary forces resulted in it being completely eviscerated.

In addition to the weakening of the former imperial armed forces, control over dissenting social and ethnic movements largely collapsed. Increasingly, competing groups within Iran sought to rigorously pursue their own goals, perceiving an opportunity to voice their opposition to central authority, and express their desire for self-rule.[24] Of these groups the Kurds, Turks, and Arabs all vied for independence or (at the very least) greater local autonomy.[25]

The Kurdish guerrillas occupied areas in western Iran that had been left abandoned following the disintegration of the Shah's armed forces. Widespread conflict began between Kurdish separatists and the army, backed by the revolutionary guards, following attempts by the central government to re-establish authority throughout Iran.[26] When the revolutionary guards encountered strong resistance from the Kurds, peace delegations were sent in by the Ayatollah, and (notwithstanding proclamations of great progress), the violence continued. One such example was upon the return of a revolutionary peace delegation which said to be "hug[e]ly successful," in spite of official reports only hours later describing "an all out attack" within western Iran by Kurdish rebels (*Guardian*, 1979d: 6). Even so, the revolutionary government was able to re-establish nominal control over the area during the period (*Guardian*, 1980: 6).

The Turkic group was perhaps the most important and possibly dangerous group of the three, with an estimated Turkish-speaking minority of 10 million people, approximately a quarter of the Iranian population at the time, seeking greater autonomy (IISS, 1979: 44). The Turkic movement was found primarily in Azerbaijan province, and was guided by the Ayatollah Shariat-Madari. Ayatollah Shariat-Madari was the second-most-important clergyman in post-revolution Iran, with his widespread support vocalized through the Muslim People's Republican Party (Cumming-Bruce, 1980: 5). When these groups challenged the central authority and the new constitution, which essentially provided for the de facto power of Ayatollah Khomeini, widespread repression resulted. Members of the Muslim People's Republican Party were targeted as a warning for the Turkic movement that resistance was to be met with a firm hand. It was also noted in the IISS (1979: 44) that the unwillingness of Ayatollah Shariat-Madari to engage in a total confrontation with the central authority limited the overall strength of the movement, and undermined its effectiveness. And despite the reluctance of Ayatollah Shariat-Madari to engage in the total confrontation with the new government the political organization attached to the Ayatollah organized a series of demonstrations, some of which turned violent, and drained military assets further in the attempt to keep Turkic populations in check (Gupte, 1980). It was from this group that the greatest possibility for destabilization was evident, particularly due to their significant numbers, creating a major vulnerability accentuated by the already inflamed Kurdish and Arab movements (Cumming-Bruce, 1980: 5).

The Arabic-speaking minority in Iran also saw the erosion of central authority during the revolution as an opportunity to push for increased autonomy in the predominantly Arab province of Khuzestan in southwest Iran (Thurgood, 1979: 5). They began a subversive movement against central government authority and were directed by their spiritual leader, Ayatollah Khaghani. It was reported that this movement was supported and sponsored by the Iraqi government under Saddam Hussein, who sought to incite the Arabs move for independence (IISS, 1980: 56–7). It is also suggested by Seale (1980: 12) that the Iraqi support extended beyond the Arabs and Arabic-speaking minorities within Iran to include the Kurds, Turkic Iranians, and the Baluchs. However, following the government crackdown involving the arrest of a large number of Arabs, along with the exile of their religious leader, the movement was left rudderless. The government crack-down was in response to a series of bomb attacks undertaken by the Arabs. It was announced by the governor-general of the province that the Ayatollah Khaghani had "been moved for his own safety" (Admiral Madani cited in the *Guardian*, 1979a: 5). Strategically, the central authority was able to undermine the Arab movement through this action as the Ayatollah had been the foremost advocate of increased autonomy (*Guardian*, 1979a: 5). Although ultimatums were issued by the movement for the return of their leader, along with ongoing threats of violence, the revolutionary government was able to curb the simmering movement through its crackdown in July, 1979 (Thurgood, 1979: 5). The Arabs continued to prosecute a low-scale independence campaign against the central authority, threatening the all important oil facilities in the region that provided the bulk of foreign exchange earnings for the Shah, and was an important source of domestically consumed oil production (*Financial Times*, 1979: 2).

Unrest did not stop with these minority groups, however, and broader social instability was created by the revolution. Military forces were required to provide security for urban centers throughout the country, which were still racked by widespread disorder in the form of protesting rural migrants seeking greater social and economic empowerment (*Los Angeles Times*, 1979b: 6; McManus, 1979: 1; *Washington Post*, 1979: 10). In one incident, revolutionary guards were confronted by 1,500 angry protestors demanding work outside the offices of Prime Minister Mehdi Bazargan, in defiance of the revolutionary government's ban on all demonstrations (*Washington Post*, 1979: 10). The social and ethnic unrest that characterized the post-revolution period amplified the military's incapacitation already caused by the revolutionary purges, requiring that it redirect its focus once again on internal security rather than on rebuilding (Randal, 1979: 14).

Moreover, domestic mobilization was inhibited by the instability brought about by the post-revolutionary turmoil, preventing the revolutionary government from utilizing its large population to its advantage, and provided for a major burden on not only the political and economic sectors, but also the already weakened military attempting to deal with openly hostile minorities.

Both Islamic extremists violently opposed to the Shah, as well as many middle class families fleeing the revolution, further impacted upon Iran's societal structure and economy. Its domestic industries were undermined through the loss of skilled workers who supplied crucial management and technical positions within the Iranian economy. The middle class began to flee the country after the revolution, leaving it with an unparalleled drain of skilled labor in Iran, unrivalled by any previous exodus. Figures purported to in Iranian sources indicated that the figure could be anywhere upwards of 100,000 (Thurgood, 1979: 7). Universities and professional sectors such as engineering and medicine experienced a significant drain as skilled workers sought more stable and liberal environments abroad (Thurgood, 1979: 7). Tehran's larger Universities lost skilled personnel after the revolution, with some staffing levels of engineering faculties diminishing by two out of every three. Reports suggest medical schools fared even worse (Thurgood, 1979: 7). This again inhibited the ability of Iran to translate its demographic indicators, derived from its large population, into power capabilities.

To compound matters further, the revolution resulted in the withdrawal of the support offered by foreign personnel who had been critical in maintaining domestic industries (particularly petroleum production) as well as military material acquisition programs. This was particularly the case after Iranian revolutionaries took over the American embassy. Islamic extremists had been mobilized during the revolution, and had been a major destabilizing force prior to the downfall of the Shah.

Islamic revolutionaries had emerged from the rural-to-urban movement and the resulting social dislocations influenced many people to turn to religion (Branigin, 1978: 8; IISS, 1978: 50). The new religious elite had immediate and wide-ranging effects on Iranian society, such as the Islamization of economics and politics (Thurgood, 1979: 7). They also had a direct impact in undermining the support felt for the regime internationally. Through religious edicts denouncing the US for its support of the Shah during his reign, and his subsequent asylum in America, Ayatollah Khomeini encouraged action to be taken against Americans within Iran (*Daily Star*, 1979: 11).

The public announcements made by Ayatollah Khomeini (cited in the *Daily Star*, 1979: 11) in the period immediately prior to the 1979 hostage saga called for "[s]chool students and theological students to extend the full force of their attacks against America and Israel, to force the America [*sic*] to extradite the criminal Shah."

As has been well documented in the past, it was revealed that the Ayatollah's revolutionary guards had allowed student protestors into the US compound (*Daily Star*, 1979: 11). This culminated in the occupation of the US embassy in Tehran and the hostage-taking of its diplomatic staff (Cumming-Bruce, 1979:1). The subsequent nonplussed response of the Iranian revolutionary government resulted in the Americans withdrawing their support, deploying two carrier forces to the Middle East, and imposing sanctions, directly undermining the military capabilities of the Iranian armed forces (IISS, 1979). As noted above, this was evident particularly in the inability of the armed forces to absorb new equipment, with the American withdrawal of support resulting in the removal of some 50–60,000 personnel.

The post-revolution period saw Iraq and the Baath party continue its process of domestic consolidation, with the final vestiges of the Iraqi Communist Party being removed from the armed forces (Kraft, 1979: 1), and the rise of Saddam Hussein to party leader and president (Hirst, 1979: 1). The Kurdish problem that had been nullified with the Algiers Agreement continued to be controlled, and to all intents and purposes, Iraq had gained a firm measure of social stability during this period.

It also sought to continue the progressive development of its domestic populace with ongoing and targeted development of the economy and education. In this period free education was introduced throughout Iraq, along with the institution of a government campaign to eradicate illiteracy (Broder, 1979: 11). It was made mandatory for all individuals between 15 and 45 years of age to learn to read and write, or face fines and possible jail time (Broder, 1979: 11).

By 1979, official statistics had over two million Iraqis taking part in this enforced literacy drive, studying in some "28,725 literacy schools manned by more then 75,000 teachers" (Cody, 1979: 26). Literacy lessons were also laced with Baathist ideology, indoctrinating the soon-to-be-literate (Cody, 1979: 26). In fact, the success of these programs was recognized by the United Nations Educational, Scientific and Cultural Organization (UNESCO), which awarded Iraq the annual prize of "the most effective literacy campaign in the world" (Cody, 1979: 26).

Consequently, it can be argued that the Iranian social instability served to further underscore the deterioration in its power position relative to Iraq, whose domestic control and mobilization of its populace was further solidified during this period. The wide-ranging effects of the Iranian revolution, such as precipitating moves by minority groups for greater autonomy, obstructing productive industrial output through strikes, and the exodus of middle-class families all contributed to this. When compared with Iraqi conditions of relative stability, one can argue that Iraq was actually able to experience a tangible power transition in their overall capabilities during the post-revolution period.

## Highly salient issues in a conflict spiral: conflict escalation to war

This meant that, unlike the constraining influence of Iran's power preponderance in the Pre-Algiers period, relations between the two countries were no longer restricted based on limited Iraqi capabilities. When correlated with the escalatory conflict cycle in their bilateral relations, Iraq's former weakness no longer prevented war. It was thus no surprise when these states again reached the precipice of war in September 1980 and the decision was made by Iraq to choose conflict over cooperation.

The examination of issues under contention thus identified the reason why these states were fighting in the lead-up to war, with the Iranian campaign towards Pan-Shi'ism resulting in a direct threat to the Iraqi state integrity, security and survival. Moreover, by viewing the changes in capabilities within the context of conflict cycles provided by interstate interaction and foreign policy reciprocity, one can better illustrate how the bilateral interaction of Iran and Iraq evolved to the point of war in 1980, and how the convergence and transition in comparative capabilities removed the constraints on the articulation of issue resolution through the use of force. The period was thus concluded with the beginning of the Iran–Iraq War on September 22, 1980.

# 6 Conclusions
## Explaining the Iran–Iraq war

This chapter serves two main purposes in order to conclude the analysis. First, I re-evaluate the main research aims and findings of this study. From these findings I develop three main conclusions regarding the relationship between the integrated approach to understanding interstate conflict escalation and war in this case. Specifically, in this research I have demonstrated the utility of issues under contention in illuminating the reasons for Iran and Iraq fighting, foreign policy reciprocity in charting the evolution of their reciprocal and conflictual interaction, and power transition in highlighting the permissive and constraining force of national power in the resolution of issues under contention.

I subsequently consider the potential value of this research in directing future studies into war causation and the integrated approach to understanding interstate conflict escalation. In doing so, I develop three embryonic questions, highlighting a possible avenue to examine other wars. I suggest that when researchers seek to answer the question of why war happens that they should ask three questions rather than one:

1 What are the issues that initially generate conflict between two states?
2 What are the contextual features of dyadic relationships which describe the evolution of conflict to war?
3 What are the permissive or constraining features that allow this conflict to evolve into war?

These questions offer future research a platform from which to evaluate other conflicts, and reinforce the utility of reconciling different approaches to the analysis of war causation.

## Research aims and main findings

The central research aim of this research has been the explanation of the cause of war, and, specifically, why the Iran–Iraq War happened when it did. In addressing this problem, I set about establishing the theoretical basis upon which to examine the Iran–Iraq War in Chapter 2. I subsequently proposed an integrated approach to understanding interstate conflict escalation utilizing issues under contention, foreign policy reciprocity, and power transition theory as explanatory tools of war's causation. I provided three interdependent theoretical expectations for each theory (outlined below), in order to assess the overall utility of this approach when empirically tested in the case of the Iran–Iraq War.

In terms of issues under contention, the theoretical examination identified that the interaction between Iran and Iraq should be directed by issues, that the most salient issues will dominate this interaction, and that either cooperative or conflictual foreign policy tools may be utilized in seeking the resolution of these issues. In addressing the expectations of foreign policy reciprocity (FPR), I identified the need for relations in the period preceding the onset of war to be characterized by an escalatory conflict cycle, interactions that were reciprocal, and when change was experienced in this interaction it was through either growth or decay. Finally, I found that power transition theory had three key expectations: (i) that a power transition occurs before the onset of war; (ii) that when relations are marked by preponderance they are generally pacific; and (iii) that relations tend to be hostile when they are characterized by power parity.

In Chapter 3, relations in the Pre-Algiers period are shown to conform with the expectations established by the integrated approach to understanding interstate conflict escalation. The interstate interaction between the two countries was oriented around the Iranian desire for regional dominance and Iraqi consolidation of central authority. From initial challenges along their shared border, relations between the two deteriorated with a conflictual and reciprocal cycle leading to the precipice of war in 1975. The examination of the dynamic power capabilities between the two states demonstrated the constraining force of the Iranian power preponderance. Indeed, the resolution through the Algiers Agreement demonstrated the Iraqi submission to Iranian dominance, making territorial concessions to the Iranians for the removal of their military support from the destabilizing Kurdish separatist movement in northern Iraq.

The cooperative tone established by the Algiers Agreement, including the resolution of the contentious and highly salient issues seen in the Pre-Algiers period, was examined in Chapter 4. This initial positive stance led to a maintained and cooperative relationship over the détente period. One moderately salient economic issue emerged for both parties revolving around OPEC pricing policies, which witnessed a cooperative and unitary stance between the two countries in seeking a resolution. This was maintained in spite of the rapid convergence in comparative power capabilities. Arguably this period reinforced the explanatory utility of the integrated approach, allowing the explanation of the shift in relations post-Algiers.

Chapter 5 proved to be significant in demonstrating the overall explanatory power of the approach implemented in this study, with the examination of the post-revolutionary period. In this chapter the expectations established through the theoretical development in Chapter 2 were clearly demonstrated. Iranian and Iraqi interstate interaction was issue-driven, with the Iranian moves towards a Pan-Shi′ism policy for the region resulting in a direct threat to the security and ongoing independence of the Iraqi state. From this point relations shifted into a competitive and escalatory conflict cycle, where each state reciprocated the actions of the other, leading the conflict to evolve to the point of war in 1980. The examination of comparative power capabilities provided a backdrop to these interactions, with Iraqi capabilities rapidly converging and transitioning with Iran. The result of which was permissive and enabling power conditions for war, allowing the Iraqi government to continue the escalation of these issues under contention in September 1980 to a full-blown war.

My findings from the empirical examination of the integrated approach to understanding interstate conflict escalation can be broken down into three distinct conclusions, as outlined below.

## *Issues under contention provided the reasons why Iran and Iraq were fighting*

In the three case study chapters (Chapters 3, 4, and 5) the examination of issues under contention allowed the identification of the most salient issues directing their interstate interaction. In Chapter 3, it was shown that the Iranian moves towards establishing regional dominance conflicted with the Iraqi desire to secure their internal legitimacy and secure control over their borders. This consequently set a stage for the initial border confrontation in 1969, setting the course of their interstate relations over the following years. The examination of foreign policy interaction, utilizing foreign policy reciprocity, also allowed this study to identify the evolution of the stakes from which these parties sought to resolve these issues.

Likewise, when Iran and Iraq reached an agreement to cease hostilities in 1975, it was clear from an examination of the outcomes that Iraq had conceded to Iranian dominance, with submission to Iranian demands for shared distribution of their common border along the Shatt al Arab. With the resolution of issues from the Pre-Algiers period, the study demonstrated intermittent moves towards joint security agreements reflecting their issue orientation, and also the emergence of a joint economic issue with the OPEC pricing division where these states sought to cooperate.

The examination of issues under contention throughout the postrevolutionary period illuminated the value of this in identifying the reasons why Iran and Iraq were fighting and what led these states to war in September 1980. This added a contextual richness to the examination of their relations, capturing what were the most important issues driving their interaction. Ayatollah Khomeini's desire to establish a Pan-Shi'ism movement within the region stimulated the threat perception the Baathist government felt towards the maintenance of their security and independence.

While it is clear that the overall utility of issues under contention is demonstrable with the identification of why these states were fighting, it would be limited without the reinforcing analysis provided through looking at the interstate interaction and foreign policy reciprocity, which allowed this study to chart the evolution and changes in the relations between these two states. This leads to the second conclusion.

***Foreign policy reciprocity allows the explanation of how relations between Iran and Iraq deteriorated to the point of war***

The broader utility of FPR was demonstrated in showing how the conflict between Iran and Iraq escalated to the point of war in 1975 and

1980. In the Pre-Algiers period of 1969–75, relations between Iran and Iraq were marked with a high degree of reciprocity, with each state resorting to increasingly hostile interactions, until the brink of full-blown war in 1974–5. Similarly, in September 1980, relations had deteriorated to the point of war, with the unilateral abrogation of cooperative treaties previously established between the two states, and the escalation of border skirmishes.

Foreign policy reciprocity builds upon issues under contention, enabling the researcher to characterize and chart the relations between these two states in terms of conflict cycles, with the interaction in this case conforming to the tenets of reciprocity theory. The broader qualitative survey established the basis upon which foreign policy reciprocity changed, so that policy reversals could be clearly identified and explained. Examining the three periods prior to the onset of hostilities in 1980 also illuminated the supporting role of power transition theory in explaining why the conflict did not escalate to war in 1975 and why it did in 1980. This leads to the third conclusion of this study.

## *Power capabilities were both permissive and constraining forces on war between Iran and Iraq*

Examining the case study through three distinct phases of interaction between Iran and Iraq also highlighted the importance of considering their relationship within a context of comparative power capabilities. The Pre-Algiers period illuminated the conflictual and escalatory interaction between these states as they contended over the Shah's projection of Iranian power within the region and created Iraqi insecurity through domestic instability; however it was their comparative power capabilities which created the conditions in which war was unnecessary for Iran and unfeasible for Iraq during a period of Iranian power preponderance.

Power transition theory clarified the structural power capabilities that acted as a restraint on both actors. The subsequent reversal in relations, shifting the interaction to a more cooperative phase after the Algiers Agreement, was prompted by Iranian power preponderance and its ability to achieve its foreign policy goals without resorting to war. Iraq, on the other hand, was inhibited by its inferior position and was forced to agree to the Algiers Agreement, accepting harsh territorial concessions in the process.

In the détente period, a cooperative relationship was maintained between these states, this was in spite of Iraq experiencing the beginning of a rapid power convergence relative to Iran. This period ended with the revolutionary change of government in Iran, which resulted in Ayatollah Khomeini emerging as supreme leader. The installation of this new revolutionary government resulted in a shift to the issues under contention, beginning a new conflict cycle between these states. This was occurring concomitantly with the Iraqi rapid power convergence and transition with Iran. Thus, in 1980 as the escalatory relations between Iran and Iraq spiraled towards war, the previously inhibiting Iranian preponderance was removed, with the relationship marked by a balanced power distribution. Iraq had experienced a rapid convergence and transition in its comparative power capabilities, removing the barrier to articulating its goals with force.

It is at this point that we can now return to answering the primary research question as to the ability of the integrated approach to understanding conflict escalation in explaining the onset of the Iran–Iraq War. It can thus be argued that the Iranian desire for Pan-Shi'ism and the Iraqi fears for domestic security and stability set a context from which a conflictual and escalatory conflict cycle emerged, with the Iraqi power transition removing all constraints on the evolution of these states interaction to war.

## Implications for the future study of war causation

These findings also offer future studies into interstate war causation a potential avenue for further research. To begin with, I have substantiated the overall utility of an integrated approach to understanding interstate conflict escalation in the case of the Iran–Iraq War. Issues under contention provide an important context for why the states begin fighting, with foreign policy reciprocity allowing the identification of patterns in how interstate conflict evolves to the point of war, and power transition theory establishes important structural constraints, in that war is more likely when relations between states have been marked by a recent power convergence and transition. From these findings I believe that we can develop three specific questions that should be considered by researchers when analyzing war causation.

1 **What are the issues that initially generate conflict between two states?**

   Issues provide an important context for which states contend, depending on the type of issue and its associated characteristics. In this case, it was ultimately shown that Iranian ideological issues which were bounded with religious and territorial values stimulated the initial conflict and lead to the emergence of security and independence issues for Iraq. These issues were highly salient for both states, and played out through a number of stakes throughout the period preceding the onset of the Iran–Iraq War.

   The ability to identify the evolution of these issues throughout the period was fundamentally linked with the second question derivative of this study when considering the evolution of conflict to war.

2 **What are the contextual features of the dyadic relationship which describe the evolution of conflict to war?**

   This reflects the importance of charting the evolution of conflict cycles, implying that states within a dyadic relationship often come to war after a period of progressively escalating hostilities. The examination of foreign policy output through this method allowed the simultaneous identification of patterns and stakes played out in their interstate interaction. Furthermore, it recognizes the role of foreign policy reciprocity in helping us chart potential phases in which power shifts might be visible and pertinent in determining the behavior of states.

   It is at this point, however, that the third question pertaining to the role of power in providing a structural inhibitor or enabler for the decision to resort to war is necessary.

3 **What are the permissive or constraining features that allow this conflict to evolve to war?**

   The two conflict cycles seen in the periods under analysis highlighted the importance of considering broader structural constraints on state behavior, with power capabilities shown to provide both a constraining and enabling force in the escalation of conflict to war in this case. The examination of dynamic power capabilities, as part of the broader integrated approach to understanding interstate conflict escalation, was invaluable in allowing this study to differentiate between the different outcomes to the interstate interaction and issue contention.

These appear to be useful questions derived from the empirical examination of Iran and Iraq, and offer a platform to evaluate other conflicts. It also serves to reinforce the importance of reconciling, albeit in a limited way, different approaches to the analysis of war. As a result, findings from this approach in forming three preliminary war indicators may well offer a basis upon which to further extend the empirical examination of this research to other cases. Researchers are likely to continue becoming more disciplined in their attempts to reconstruct and clarify both past and new approaches, in order to answer the enduring question: why war? In this research, I hope to have made a contribution towards this goal.

# Appendix 1

*Table 1.1* Comparative total population (Tpop)

| Year | Iran (000s) | % change | Iraq (000s) | % change | Iraqi pop.per | Iran:Iraq Tpop ratio |
|---|---|---|---|---|---|---|
| 1970 | 28705 | – | 9440 | – | 32.88 | 3.04 |
| 1971 | 29484 | 2.71 | 9750 | 3.28 | 33.06 | 3.02 |
| 1972 | 30284 | 2.71 | 10074 | 3.32 | 33.26 | 3.00 |
| 1973 | 31106 | 2.71 | 10413 | 3.36 | 33.47 | 2.98 |
| 1974 | 31951 | 2.71 | 10765 | 3.38 | 33.69 | 2.96 |
| 1975 | 32818 | 2.71 | 11124 | 3.33 | 33.89 | 2.95 |
| 1976 | 33709 | 2.71 | 11505 | 3.42 | 34.13 | 2.92 |
| 1977 | 35025 | 3.90 | 12030 | 4.56 | 34.34 | 2.91 |
| 1978 | 36393 | 3.90 | 12405 | 3.11 | 34.08 | 2.93 |
| 1979 | 37814 | 3.90 | 12821 | 3.35 | 33.90 | 2.94 |
| 1980 | 39291 | 3.90 | 13238 | 3.25 | 33.69 | 2.96 |

*Table 1.2* Comparative percentage urban population (%Upop)

| Year | Iran (%) | % change | Iraq (%) | % change | Iraqi pop. per | Iran:Iraq % Upop ratio |
|---|---|---|---|---|---|---|
| 1970 | 21.01 | – | 34.70 | – | 165.17 | 0.60 |
| 1971 | 21.92 | 4.36 | 36.30 | 4.62 | 165.58 | 0.60 |
| 1972 | 22.12 | 0.88 | 37.97 | 4.60 | 171.69 | 0.58 |
| 1973 | 22.60 | 2.19 | 39.70 | 4.55 | 175.65 | 0.56 |
| 1974 | 24.54 | 8.58 | 41.50 | 4.52 | 169.08 | 0.59 |
| 1975 | 26.36 | 7.42 | 43.41 | 4.59 | 164.62 | 0.60 |
| 1976 | 28.07 | 6.46 | 45.35 | 4.47 | 161.54 | 0.61 |
| 1977 | 31.58 | 12.51 | 46.87 | 3.35 | 148.38 | 0.67 |
| 1978 | 32.61 | 3.23 | 49.12 | 4.80 | 150.64 | 0.66 |
| 1979 | 33.59 | 3.00 | 51.36 | 4.56 | 152.92 | 0.65 |
| 1980 | 34.58 | 2.95 | 53.76 | 4.65 | 155.45 | 0.64 |

*Table 1.3* Comparative urban population (Upop)

| Year | Iran (000s) | % change | Iraq (000s) | % change | Iraqi pop.per | Iran:Iraq Upop ratio |
|---|---|---|---|---|---|---|
| 1970 | 6031 |  | 3276 |  | 54.31 | 1.84 |
| 1971 | 6465 | 7.19 | 3540 | 8.05 | 54.75 | 1.82 |
| 1972 | 6699 | 3.61 | 3826 | 8.07 | 57.11 | 1.75 |
| 1973 | 7032 | 4.97 | 4135 | 8.07 | 58.80 | 1.70 |
| 1974 | 7843 | 11.53 | 4468 | 8.05 | 56.96 | 1.75 |
| 1975 | 8654 | 10.34 | 4829 | 8.07 | 55.80 | 1.79 |
| 1976 | 9464 | 9.35 | 5218 | 8.05 | 55.13 | 1.81 |
| 1977 | 11064 | 16.90 | 5639 | 8.06 | 50.96 | 1.96 |
| 1978 | 11868 | 7.26 | 6094 | 8.06 | 51.34 | 1.94 |
| 1979 | 12702 | 7.02 | 6586 | 8.07 | 51.85 | 1.92 |
| 1980 | 13588 | 6.97 | 7117 | 8.06 | 52.37 | 1.90 |

Total and urban population data is sourced from the Correlates of War (COW) Project. Total population is determined by the number of residents within a state, with COW analysts utilizing a *de facto* measurement. A de facto measurement results in the assessment of all residents within a state's borders, while a de jure measurement only measures those that are legal residents (for more information see Singer *et al.*, 1972). The COW data was largely derivative from United Nations statistics. Both the WDI and the Military Balance provide figures for total population and are congruent with COW figures.

Urban population is determined by the number of people living in cities over 100,000 (Singer *et al.*, 1972). The COW methodology assesses urban population, as opposed to a more contemporary urban agglomeration method. Urban agglomeration differs from the urban population method in that it figures in both the city proper population and its surrounding suburbs. Obviously, with the shifting dynamics of urbanization in developed and less developed countries this method could provide for a better determination of the degree of population development. Despite the value of this approach figures are still largely not available, especially historical data in less developed countries, this fact is reflected in many international assessments.

In fact, many indices do not provide any, or very limited, data relating to urban population. This point is highlighted through an examination of both the WDI and Military Balance, with neither index providing a comprehensive list of Iran and Iraq's urban population. So, in spite of its weaknesses, COW indices do allow a limited assessment of the comparative urban population of Iran and Iraq.

# Appendix 2

*Table 2.1* Comparative GDP (in millions of US dollars, based on 1990 market prices)

| Year | Iran (10⁶) | % change | Iraq (10⁶) | % change | Iraqi GDP % | GDP ratio |
|---|---|---|---|---|---|---|
| 1970 | 55989 |  | 11826 |  | 21.12 | 4.73 |
| 1971 | 62900 | 12.34 | 12634 | 6.83 | 20.09 | 4.97 |
| 1972 | 73141 | 16.28 | 12156 | −3.78 | 16.62 | 6.01 |
| 1973 | 79409 | 8.57 | 14437 | 18.76 | 18.18 | 5.50 |
| 1974 | 84669 | 6.62 | 15781 | 9.30 | 18.64 | 5.36 |
| 1975 | 89289 | 5.45 | 18084 | 14.59 | 20.25 | 4.93 |
| 1976 | 104409 | 16.93 | 21719 | 20.1 | 20.8 | 4.80 |
| 1977 | 103256 | −1.1 | 22193 | 2.18 | 21.49 | 4.65 |
| 1978 | 91844 | −11.1 | 26343 | 18.7 | 28.68 | 3.48 |
| 1979 | 84521 | −7.97 | 33019 | 25.34 | 39.07 | 2.55 |
| 1980 | 73701 | −12.8 | 32077 | −2.85 | 43.52 | 2.29 |

*Table 2.2* Comparative GDP per capita (in US dollars, based on 1990 market prices)

| Year | Iran | % change | Iraq | % change | Iraqi GDP per capita % | GDP ratio |
|---|---|---|---|---|---|---|
| 1970 | 1950.5 |  | 1253 |  | 64.23 | 1.55 |
| 1971 | 2133.4 | 9.37 | 1296 | 3.43 | 60.74 | 1.64 |
| 1972 | 2415.2 | 13.21 | 1207 | −6.88 | 49.96 | 2.00 |
| 1973 | 2552.9 | 5.70 | 1386 | 14.9 | 54.31 | 1.84 |
| 1974 | 2650 | 3.80 | 1466 | 5.73 | 55.32 | 1.80 |
| 1975 | 2720.7 | 2.67 | 1626 | 10.9 | 59.75 | 1.67 |
| 1976 | 3097.4 | 13.84 | 1888 | 16.12 | 60.95 | 1.64 |
| 1977 | 2948.1 | −4.82 | 1845 | −2.28 | 62.58 | 1.59 |
| 1978 | 2523.7 | −14.4 | 2124 | 15.11 | 84.15 | 1.18 |
| 1979 | 2235.2 | −11.4 | 2575 | 21.28 | 115.2 | 0.86 |
| 1980 | 1875.8 | −16.1 | 2423 | −5.91 | 129.2 | 0.77 |

Data relating to GDP was sourced from the United Nations Statistics Division. The GDP figures are based on 1990 market prices, and displayed in US dollars. This measure is an aggregate of all production derived from resident institutional units including taxes, and minus any subsidies. It also includes a measure of the "sum of the final uses of goods and services (all uses except intermediate consumption) measured in purchasers' prices, less the value of imports of goods and services, or the sum of primary incomes distributed by resident producer units."

The choice to utilize UN estimates of GDP at 1990 market prices, listed in US dollars, was made under the auspices of two main reasons. First, the congruence in economic data relating Iran and Iraq was very limited, with estimates from alternative sources often being in differing unit measures (like the Iraqi dinar), which would have inhibited the comparative analysis of these two countries. This was particularly evident in the assessment conducted by both the WDI and the Military Balance. Second, the availability of alternative measures, such as GDP PPP, or GDP in current prices, or even GDP growth rates, has not been consistently published for either of these countries during the temporal period under examination. This includes not only WDI and the Military Balance, but also the OECD and IMF which also provide large repositories of economic data.

# Appendix 3

*Table 3.1* Comparative military expenditures (MilEx)

| Year | Iran | % change | Iraq | % change | Iraqi MilEx % | MilEx ratio |
|---|---|---|---|---|---|---|
| 1970 | 735313 |  | 251470 |  | 34.19 | 2.92 |
| 1971 | 735313 | 0 | 427398 | 69.95 | 58.12 | 1.72 |
| 1972 | 1087788 | 47.93 | 459597 | 7.53 | 42.25 | 2.36 |
| 1973 | 1814697 | 66.82 | 658068 | 43.18 | 36.26 | 2.75 |
| 1974 | 4658080 | 156.68 | 1429055 | 117.15 | 30.67 | 3.25 |
| 1975 | 6667751 | 43.14 | 1591601 | 11.37 | 23.87 | 4.18 |
| 1976 | 7746860 | 16.18 | 1760921 | 10.63 | 22.73 | 4.39 |
| 1977 | 7972585 | 2.91 | 2008127 | 14.03 | 25.18 | 3.97 |
| 1978 | 9137992 | 14.61 | 1987809 | −1.01 | 21.75 | 4.59 |
| 1979 | 5462930 | −40.21 | 2675245 | 34.58 | 48.97 | 2.04 |
| 1980 | 3386907 | −38.00 | 3386780 | 26.59 | 99.99 | 1.00 |

*Table 3.2* Comparative military personnel (MilPer)

| Year | Iran | % change | Iraq | % change | Iraqi MilPer % | MilPer ratio |
|---|---|---|---|---|---|---|
| 1970 | 245 |  | 95 |  | 38.77 | 2.57 |
| 1971 | 255 | 4.08 | 105 | 10.52 | 41.17 | 2.42 |
| 1972 | 265 | 3.92 | 105 | 0 | 39.62 | 2.52 |
| 1973 | 285 | 7.54 | 105 | 0 | 36.84 | 2.71 |
| 1974 | 310 | 8.77 | 110 | 4.76 | 35.48 | 2.81 |
| 1975 | 385 | 24.19 | 155 | 40.90 | 40.25 | 2.48 |
| 1976 | 420 | 9.09 | 190 | 22.58 | 45.23 | 2.21 |
| 1977 | 350 | −16.66 | 140 | −26.31 | 40 | 2.5 |
| 1978 | 350 | 0 | 362 | 158.57 | 103.42 | 0.96 |
| 1979 | 415 | 18.57 | 444 | 22.65 | 106.98 | 0.93 |
| 1980 | 305 | −26.50 | 430 | −3.15 | 140.98 | 0.70 |

Data relating to both military personnel and expenditure is derivative of the Correlates of War (COW) Project (see Singer *et al.*, 1972). The military personnel variable measures the size of a state's armed forces under the command of "the national government intended for use against foreign adversaries, and held ready for combat as of January 1 of the referent year" (Singer *et al.*, 1972). These COW figures are derived primarily from the US Arms Control and Disarmament Agency for the periods between 1961 until 1993. It is also supplemented, where necessary, by the International Institute of Strategic Studies data. The other key comparative indices utilized to compare the COW data, the World Development Indicators, did not possess military personnel data. It is based on quantifying only those troops under the control of national governments. Troops outside central administrative command are not counted within this data.

One particularly important weakness of this data is that the assessment of military personnel levels are undertaken at the beginning of each year and may not be able to reflect rapid changes through mobilization for wars. As Singer *et al.*, (1972) also acknowledge, precise figures cannot always be accurately quantified due to some states utilizing defence personnel levels as leverage in foreign policy bargaining.

The military expenditure variable is defined as the "total military budget for a given state for a given year" (Singer *et al.*, 1972). When determining this figure COW analysts differentiated the appropriations for military and non-military sources, without this differentiation the assessment of military expenditures would be subject to over-estimation, skewing the analysis (Singer *et al.*, 1972).

A particular problem often associated with the determination of military expenditure is currency conversion. Expenditures are normally published in the national currency of the respective country. This is reflected in many assessments of military expenditures, including the Military Balance. The COW project, however, utilized a standard unit, for the period under analysis this is the US dollar. The benefit of this approach is clearly apparent, allowing the comparative assessment of military expenditures in countries that do not use the same currency. The COW project utilized the International Monetary Fund in determining the respective conversions (Singer *et al.*, 1972).

# Notes

## 1 An integrated approach to understanding interstate conflict escalation: introduction

1 See, for example, Kaldor (2005; 2006); and Kober (2005).
2 For example, Juhasz (2007); Claes (2005); Verrastro *et al.* (2004); and Morse (2004).
3 See, for example, Fürtig (2007); Layne (2007); Lieven *et al.*, (2007); and Cole (2006).
4 For other examples of causes of war see Colaresi (2004); Crescenzi and Enterline (2001); Jervis (1999); Leng (1998); Hensel (1999); and Hudson and Vore (1995).
5 For examples of balance of power arguments see Reus-Smit (2004); Porter (2005); and Paul *et al.* (2004).
6 See, for example, Moul (2003); Lemke and Werner (1996); and Siverson and Sullivan (1983).
7 Power transition arguments are notable in Lee (2006); Kreft (2006); and DiCicco and Levy (1999).
8 See Hebron *et al.* (2007); and Parsi (2005).
9 Several such examples can be seen in Thompson (2006): 1–22, and William Wohlforth, "Unipolar Stability," *Harvard International Review*, 29(1), (Spring 2007): 44–8.
10 One such example can be seen in Volgy and Imwalle (1995).
11 One need only look at a snapshot of post-9/11 articles relating to this conflict to demonstrate the depth of research that is being maintained within this area. For example, Djerejian (2006); Nofal (2004); Ben-Yehuda and Sandler (2003); and Slater (2002).

## 2 An integrated approach to understanding interstate conflict escalation: theoretical foundations

1 Perhaps reflecting the increasing focus on norms derived from social constructivism.
2 For example, see Diehl (1992); Luard (1987); Rosenau (1967); and Vasquez (1993).
3 For example, see Hensel (2001); and Vasquez (1983).
4 For more details, see Holsti (1991).

5 See for further information on the value of both of these approaches Rosenau (1966); Vasquez (1983); Diehl (1992); Hensel *et al.* (2008); and Holsti (1991).
6 Luard (1987) also discussed this in his classification of different temporal periods characterized by conflict over particular issues. One such example is in his age of sovereignty, between 1648 and 1789, where states fought over the balance of power between themselves, consolidating their own state power, while attempting to prevent other powers from encroaching upon them.
7 Luard (1987) takes this argument one step further describing the current period, from 1917 onwards as being characterized as an age of ideology. This period has been characterized broadly by issues of ideology, and more specifically conflicting ideologies. He draws on the example of the competition seen between totalitarian dictatorships, autocratic governments, socialist forces and Western democracies that led to World War I and World War II. More recently, in the post–World War II period the conflict shifted to being orientated between the two superpowers and their associated international alliances.
8 Bercovitch and Jackson (1997) also refer to state integrity when discussing other common issues stimulating conflict. They broaden this idea to also include simple interference into the domestic affairs of another state.
9 For further information with regard to the theory of reciprocity see also Colaresi (2004); Lebovic (2003); Leng (1998); Druckman (1998); Rajmaira (1997); and Vasquez (1995).
10 It is important to note, for the sake of thoroughness, that reciprocity can also be broken down into two key types: contingent and equivalent. Contingent reciprocity implies that actors within a relationship will specifically respond based on the others actors' behavior. Contingent reciprocity implies that an actor would then return cooperation for cooperation, or conversely, defection for defection (Keohane, 1986: 5–6). Equivalent reciprocity holds that an actor will respond in like to another actor's exchange, and this may be done through relationships marked by equality or inequality. An example among equals could be that both states agree to contribute an equal amount towards and international organization protecting their interests. Within a relationship marked by inequality, for instance a patron–client relationship, the exchanges would then be mutually valued but not necessarily of the same comparative value (Keohane, 1986: 6).
11 According to Leeds and Davis (1999: 17) the decision to undertake or initiate war is the "culmination of a process of interaction." Their findings support the supposition that international relations are interactive, and a state's foreign policy behavior is formulated within the context of the expected behavior of their counterparts (Leeds and Davis, 1999: 18).
12 This also reflects the conceptual basis of Crescenzi and Enterline (2001), who explore the conflict and cooperative components that characterize dyadic relationships over extended periods of time. The empirical examination undertaken by Crescenzi and Enterline (2001: 409) reinforces the role that historical processes play in the dyadic relations of two states.
13 This idea of ongoing interaction forms a key element of the iterated prisoners dilemma, with states more likely to resort to cooperation, as opposed to defection, if their immediate behavior is considered in relation to possible future interactions.
14 A number of factors can be attributed to influencing the initiation of change from one type of behavior to another. Although the emphasis of this study is on how the nature of change is influenced by power capability distribution and issues under contention between two states, it is important to recognize that change in

reciprocal relations is not limited to considerations of power, and can indeed be stimulated by a range of other factors. Some are developed by Rasler (2000: 701) who contends that conflict de-escalation of protracted conflicts can be stimulated through factors such as external and internal shocks, new policy strategies, third-party pressure, political entrepreneurs, and policy control. This is also recognized in Clark and Reed (2005) who argue that states can choose to change their policy behavior through a process of substitution, influenced by a range of factors including political and economic conditions. For theoretical thoroughness, it is important to recognize that these factors all contribute to changes in policy direction. Although policy reciprocity can provide an important guiding force for the interactions of states, it is not the sole determinant of behavior, and is, as such, subject to its own limitations in explaining the interaction of states. Moreover, the argument regarding temporal change is also extended by Ward and Rajimaira (1992), who argue that reciprocity can be both from a short-term action-reaction perspective, or over a longer period allowing for norms to be developed.

15 Perhaps the most elaborate definition of foreign policy is proposed by Goldmann (1982: 234–5) who argues that policy is characterized by four key components:

1 Policy: an agent's line of action with regard to an object. This component of the definition reflects the breadth of policy and its operational application. It involves an agent (in this case a state), undertaking a specific action or inaction, towards some specific object. The term "object" is utilized by Goldmann to reflect the ability of policy to be directed at either another actor (like a state or NGO) or a specific issue area (such as trade policy or strategic weapons limitations).

2 Line of action: the agent does alpha whenever beta obtains; beta will occur more than once or a restricted number of times. Line of action can be translated to reflect the interdependence of action and outcome. An actor then undertakes a particular course of action, with an intended outcome. Once it is achieved, the actor will repeat the action to replicate the intended result. An action thus immediately implies tangible and actualized decisions by an actor towards some given outcome. This may be more broadly defined to include the desire to act a certain way within a specified situation.

3 Verbalized policy: a line of action that an agent declares he is following or intends to follow with regard to an object. Verbalized policy is identified as being solely in the domain of articulated actor declarations. This reflects a line of action pursued by the actor which is described—usually in detail—before the event occurs and usually reflects strategic decision making. It will entail a specific formulation of an intended action and outcome expected by the actor.

4 Non-verbalized policy: a line of action followed by an agent with regard to an object. Non-verbalized policy is not articulated in declaratory statements by the actor, and can be "specified by The Observer and not by the agent." Non-verbalized policy, unlike the strategic pre planned nature of verbalized policy, is typically characterized through some form of generalization about the actors' past actions or behaviour.

16 According to Hudson and Vore (1995: 226) the focus of context/input analysis comes from a psychosocial context based on five key aspects including individual characteristics, perceptions, society and culture, the polity, and the international system.

17 The analysis of foreign policy decision making is focused on both small and large group dynamics and how decisions are arrived at, as well as the cognitive development of tasks within that group (Hudson and Vore, 1995: 223–5). It involves the analysis of individual foreign policy decisions, and the delineation of patterns in the way change and uncertainty is dealt with. For examples of this approach, see Kuperman (2006); Mintz et al. (1997); and Hudson and Vore (1995).
18 This definition focuses on the chosen policy of the state in terms of its articulated domestic and foreign policies that can be linked to actions undertaken by that state. It does not seek to classify and code the all the possible preferences that may be evident in policy process analysis (Lamborn, 1985).
19 For a more detailed review of the definition of power see Jablonsky (1997); Treverton and Jones (2005); Hocking and Smith (1990); and Wheatsheaf et al. (1982).
20 For examples of balance of power arguments see Reus-Smit (2004); Porter (2005); Paul et al. (2004); Horowitz (2001); Niou and Ordeshook (1986); Deutsch and Singer (1964); Siverson and Sullivan (1983); and Geller (1993).
21 Power preponderance arguments can be seen in Lemke and Werner (1996); Geller, (1993); and Weede (1976).
22 Power transition arguments are notable in Lee (2006); Kreft (2006); DiCicco and Levy, (1999); Lemke (1997); de Soysa et al. (1997); and Organski and Kugler (1980).
23 For examples of hegemonic stability see Volgy and Imwalle (1995); Miller (2001); and Thompson (1986).
24 For example, see Moul (2003); Lemke (1997); and Lee (2006).
25 For example, see Bremer (1992); or Doran (1989).
26 Geller (1993: 174) also supports the proposition of Bremer (1992), arguing that "when one side has a clear military advantage, the weaker cannot afford to fight and the stronger does not have to in order to achieve its goals."
27 For example, see Woosang (2002); Reed (2003); Morton and Starr, (2001); and de Soysa et al. (1997).
28 A power threshold method will be employed in the assessment raw data, originally identified by Organski and Kugler in their pioneering study of power transition theory in *The War Ledger* (1980). They argued that states, or systems, with a power differential of 20 percent or more are characterized by a power preponderance relationship. Two states in which the power differential is characterized by a difference in size less then this are to be considered equal in power, or converging to parity. Obviously if there is a shift in their comparative positions, with one state surpassing the others national power, a power transition has occurred. The power threshold of 20 percent is used as an indicative guide to the power relationship that exists, helping establish a basic understanding of the power distribution that is evident both from a relative and comparative perspective. Power conversion factors will be used to supplement this assessment.
29 DiCicco and Levy (1999: 681) further attenuate this arguing that this dominant power, be it a single state or group of states "achieves its preeminent position in the international hierarchy through a process of rapid economic development that is driven by industrialization."
30 For example, see Lemke (1997: 24) who proposes that this new dominant state will establish an international order from which it will gain economic, prestige, and security.

31 Dynamic power balances can also be further broken down into two main categories: power transitions and power shifts (Geller, 1993). Power transitions are where the power distribution between two states, or opposing blocs of states, exhibits a reversal in their relative power position. Power shifts occur when there is a convergence or divergence in the comparative level of power distribution between two states, or opposing blocs of states (DiCicco and Levy, 1999).
32 See DiCicco and Levy (1999); Geller (1993); and Lemke (1997).
33 Although, unlike traditionalists, Woosang (2002) extends the application of the theory to take into account alliances.
34 A further indicator is offered within the COW project, referred to as industrial capabilities. This indicator seeks to demonstrate the iron and steel consumption, and primary energy consumption of states. Although having some value in terms of assessing the industrial capacity of the state, I believe that it is flawed for the post–World War II international dynamics. One such example demonstrating this approach can be found in the "Great Leap Forward" in China, where the Chinese sought to dramatically increase the country's agricultural and steel production. In this period, many small backyard furnaces used "scrap" metal sourced from kitchen utensils to agricultural implements, and enabled the Chinese to dramatically increase the amount of steel produced. However, this often lacked any real usable quality and deprived the Chinese of important materials formally used for productive output. Besides this fact, in terms of military capabilities the production of iron or steel has limited qualitative significance as many smaller states, such as states being analyzed in this case, now source their military equipment and hardware from a larger state. Hence, a more accurate indicator of a domestic capability being able to be utilized for military purposes would be GDP or GNP, which can be used to determine either direct access to resources (or potential to access them). For more information on the vast impact of the Cultural Revolution and the Great Leap Forward, see Robinson (1970); Esherick et al. (2006); and Teiwes and Sun (1999).
35 The COW indices provide a broad basis of capability assessment, with military and demographic data playing an important role in the determination of national power. The COW Composite Index remains one of the most widely used bases for determining national power. For example, see Chan (2005); Casetti (2003); de Soysa et al. (1997); and Schampel (1993).
36 The two most common methods of measuring demographic indicators are total population and urban population, presented in the COW Project, and utilized in this study (Singer et al., 1972).
37 Derivative of the COW quantitative basis.
38 For examples of its use in the assessment of national capabilities, see Lee (2006); Nye (2002/2003); de Soysa et al. (1997); and Lemke (1997).
39 Lebovic (1985) suggest the potency of economic capabilities comes from their potential translation into overall power capabilities, be it through direct translation into military capabilities, or for other means. Indeed, Lee (2006: 60) maintains the predominance of military power in his assessment of power capability and shifts, although he does note, that "wealth underpins military power, shifts in economic power in the long run lead to parallel changes in military balance." While Emilio Casetti (2003) suggests that economic capabilities, be it GNP or GDP, provide a direct index of the quality of a population. Moreover, it can provide the "best "overall" index of military, economic and political power, as the sum of goods and services that a county is capable of producing supports any mix of military,

economic, and political collective actions in pursuit of power goals" (Casetti, 2003: 663).
40 For more details, see de Soysa *et al.* (1997); Casetti (2003); and Lee (2006).
41 One such example can be seen in the Iranian military expenditures. It will be demonstrated that although Iranian expenditures reached four times that of Iraq's in 1978, this did not translate into realized power as Iran was unable to efficiently and effectively absorb this new equipment into its forces. The introduction of power conversion factors reflects a subtle shift in contemporary scholarly debate on the accurate assessment of national power. Increasingly, traditional approaches to the analysis of national power through broad based quantitative indicators are being broadened to allow the incorporation of a more nuanced approach. This can be seen, for example, in Chan (2005) who focuses not only on the use of the COW Project or Economic Capabilities (such as GDP and GDP per capita) in the assessment of national power, but also from Kevin Sweeney's composite index of hard and soft power. Sweeney (cited in Chan, 2005: 694) includes non-traditional measures of national power such as tourist visits, number of foreign exchange students hosted, radios, and televisions, amongst others. Chan (2005) clearly points to the importance of shifting beyond traditional approaches to the measurement of power capabilities, particularly with regard to broad-based quantitative indicators, towards qualitative analysis illuminating the nuances in national capabilities. Nye (2003: 549) reaffirms this argument in a more recent publication, purporting to the shift in the measure of national power, with the incorporation of both hard and soft power. Hard power relates to traditional measure such as large armies, populations, or even economies, and soft to the force of its moral, cultural, and ideological power. Although Nye does, nonetheless, recognize the intractable importance of hard power determinants in some situations, one of which would be the exercise of force
42 For example, the Indo-Pakistani War in 1971 (between 3 and 16 December 1971). For more information, see Sisson and Rose (1990); Zaheer (1994); and Palit (1972).
43 Such as the Six Day War (June 5–10, 1967) or the Yom Kippur War (between October 6 and 28). For example, see Dupuy (1978).
44 According to Hiro (1989: 1) the both the direct and indirect damaged caused by hostilities is "an astronomical figure of $1,190 billion."
45 This expectation also finds resonance in the study by Joshua S. Goldstein and Jon C. Pevehouse (1997) who test the degree of reciprocity in the Bosnian conflict.

## 3 The pre-Algiers period: phase 1 of Iran–Iraq relations

1 It has been suggested by Phebe Marr (1970), however, that a coup may not have actually occurred. Rather, a conspiracy may have been uncovered, which gave the Baathist regime the opportunity to eliminate some of its internal opponents and redirect the focus on external threats posed by Iran. Nevertheless, the moves by Iraq were clearly seen as escalating the conflict cycle that was occurring between itself and Iran.
2 Cooley (1970: 2) contends that Iran's increasing interference in the affairs of Iraq, including its support of the Kurdish guerrilla movement, were linked with its desire to extend its influence in the area following the removal of British forces.

3 This shift in British foreign policy resulted from the decline in its projection of power within the Middle East region seen post-Suez (Mawby, 2005; Ashton, 1997). The removal of British troops in 1971 from the Persian Gulf region marked the end of a 150-year presence in the region. It also ended the British guardianship over smaller oil-rich states of the region including Bahrain and Qatar (IISS, 1971; *Daily Star*, 1973: 2). See also Karsh,1987–88).
4 These Islands were claimed by the Ruler of Ras al Khaimah, and had been under their administration.
5 Iraq argued that Britain had been in collusion with Iranian expansionist designs, due not only to the timing of their withdrawal and the Iranian occupation of the Islands, but also in their acquiescence to the Iranian occupation. Reports had emerged during this period reinforcing the British and American blessing for Iran to expand its security role in the Gulf, with the defence acquisition program underwriting Iran's capability to do so (Szulc, 1971: 1). This included an extensive supply of military materials ranging from US fighters to British tanks and ships (see Szulc, 1971: 1).
6 IISS (1971: 42) notes that in 1971, following the occupation of these Islands in the Strait of Hormuz, the Iraqi response was the "harassment and deportation of Iranians living in Iraq . . . tens of thousands, many long-standing Iraqi dwellers, were dumped on Iran's borders." This was also reported in the *Daily Star*(a) (1972: 3); and in the *Daily Star*(a) (1972: 1).
7 Following their successful bid for independence from Britain in 1961, Kuwait had been subject to claims by the then Iraqi premier Major-General Abdul Karim Kassem, that Kuwait was an integral part of Iraq (*New York Times*, 1973: 6). Although the result of the clashes at the time had seen the British intervene (subject to their treaty of protection) with Kuwait's independence maintained, the exact boundary between the two countries remained ambiguous (*New York Times*, 1973: 6; Hoagland, 1973: 1).
8 For more details, see the report from the 2250th United Nations Security Council Meeting, October 15, 1980.
9 Although a UN-brokered cease-fire was instituted on October 22, 1973, it was not until October 28 that an effective end came to the hostilities. On this day, the Israeli defence minister, Moshe Dayan, announced to the Knesset that the Americans had threatened to halt their airlift of military supplies for the Israel Defense Force, should it not allow the Egyptian Third Army food and water supplies. It ended the stand-off regarding the fate of the entrapped Egyptian military units. For more information see Sagan (1979).
10 Some theorists would argue that this was not characteristic of a usual policy reversal due to the limited temporal period in action, no long-term binding agreements influencing and maintaining this shift, a swift return to conflict (not a sustained peace or cooperation), and the influence of external events on this shift. I would concur, with this change in behavior more characteristic of a temporary interruption to their reciprocal interactivity, given that bilateral relations swiftly returned to conflict subsequent to the conclusion of the October war.
11 See, for example, *The Times* (1974); Caputo (1974: 3); *Chicago Tribune* (1974: 15); *Chicago Tribune* (1974: 4); *Washington Post* (1974: 19); *New York Times* (1974a: 8); and *Los Angeles Times* (1974a: 2).
12 For further information regarding the skirmishes during February 1974, see *Daily Star* (1974b: 1); Permanent Representative of Iran to the United Nations, March 6, 1974; Deputy Permanent Representative of Iraq, February 12, 1974; *Daily Star*

## Notes 125

(1974a: 1); *The Times* (1974); *Los Angeles Times* (1974a: 2); *Los Angeles Times* (1974c: 11); and *Los Angeles Times* (1974d: 6).

13 For example, see Permanent Representative of Iran, March 6, 1974; Deputy Permanent Representative of Iraq, February 12, 1974; *New York Times* (1974b: 3); *Los Angeles Times* (1974d: 6); *Chicago Tribune* (1974: 9); and *New York Times* (1974c: 8).
14 For more details, see Permanent Representative of Iraq, September 4, 1974.
15 More details relating to Iranian accusations can be found in the report, Permanent Representative of Iran to the United Nations, September 6, 1974.
16 Further recriminations were outlined in the report given to the United Nations, see Permanent Representative of Iraq to the United Nations, December 18, 1974.
17 For more information, see Appendix 1, Table 1.1 Comparative total population.
18 See Appendix 1, Table 1.1 Comparative total population.
19 See Appendix 1, Table 1.3 Comparative urban population.
20 See Appendix 1, Table 1.3 Comparative urban population.
21 For more information see Appendix 1, Table 1.3 Comparative urban population.
22 See Appendix 2, Table 2.1 Comparative GDP.
23 See Appendix 2, Table 2.1 Comparative GDP.
24 For more information see Appendix 2, Table 2.1 Comparative GDP.
25 See Appendix 2, Table 2.2 Comparative GDP per capita.
26 For more information see Appendix 2, Table 2.2 Comparative GDP per capita.
27 For more information see Appendix 3, Table 3.1 Comparative military expenditure.
28 See Appendix 3, Table 3.1 Comparative military expenditure.
29 See Appendix 3, Table 3.1 Comparative military expenditure.
30 For more information see Appendix 3, Table 3.1 Comparative military expenditure.
31 See Appendix 3, Table 3.2 Comparative military personnel.
32 For more information see Appendix 3, Table 3.2 Comparative military personnel.
33 It has also been noted that resources were siphoned off from domestic development projects, assisting the industrialization and modernization of the country to fund the rapid expansion in expenditure allocated to the military.
34 For a more comprehensive review of the expansion seen in the Iranian material acquisition see IISSa (1970/71); IISSb (1971/72); IISSc (1973/74); IISSd (1974/75); and IISSe (1975/76).
35 See, for example, *New York Times* (1972c: 3); *Washington Post* (1972: 14); *New York Times* (1972b: 3); *Daily Star* (1972d: 1); *Daily Star* (1972e: 1).
36 For more information see Hoagland (1972: 8); *Washington Post* (1972: 22); *New York Times* (1972d: 12); *Chicago Tribune* (1972); and *New York Times* (1972a: 44). See, for more information regarding the 1970 peace agreement, *New York Times* (1970a: 8); *Los Angeles Times* (1970: 19); Schmidt (1970: 8); Lewis (1970: 32); and *New York Times* (1970b: 5).
37 Kurdish sources went as far as to estimate some 80–90 percent of Iraqi ground forces were operating in Kurdish areas during 1974 (see Hirst, 1974: 5).
38 In 1974, the entire Iraqi Armed Forces was composed of 110,000 personnel. Refer to Appendix 1, Table 1.2 Comparative military personnel chart.
39 This was particularly noted in Morris (1977: 18), who suggested that Iraq, "with a population of 12 million[,] ... is underpopulated" causing major manpower issues for the expansion of the economy.
40 See also Melloan (1973: 26); and Spanier (1972: 14).
41 For more information on the "White Revolution" see Walz (1963: 210); Morris (1967: 4); and Friendly (1969: 16).

126  *Notes*

42  For more information see Vis Raein (1973: 3); or *The Times* (1971:8).
43  The broader impact of this program is detailed in *The Times* (1971:8).
44  The Kurds were estimated to be roughly 20 percent of the population. See Stork (1981) for more details.
45  A theoretical line, dividing rivers and gulfs by equally separating its control between the two neighboring countries. See, for more information, *Daily Star* (1974c: 1).
46  See, for example, Martin (1969: 4); *Washington Post* (1969: 16); and Durdin (1969: 2).

## 4  The détente period: phase 2 of Iran–Iraq relations

1  This was stimulated by attempts to have the Persian Gulf renamed the Arabian Gulf. It included Saudi Arabia, Iraq, Kuwait, Bahrain, the United Arab Emirates, Qatar, and Oman (*Los Angeles Times*, 1976: 4).
2  Ayatollah Khomeini had resided in Iraq from 1963 up until this point in January 1978, following his exile from Iran. He was then to spend several months at the end of 1978 and beginning of 1979 in France, following being expelled from Iraq. More details of his time in France can be seen in Randal (1978: 18).
3  See Appendix 1, Table 1.1 Comparative total population.
4  For more information see Appendix 1, Table 1.1 Comparative total population.
5  See Appendix 1, Table 1.3 Comparative urban population.
6  See Appendix 2, Table 2.1 Comparative GDP.
7  For more information see Appendix 2, Table 2.1 Comparative GDP.
8  Clearly, however, there is still a significant gap between their comparative GDP per capita, with an Iranian advantage of 1.18:1.
9  For more information see Appendix 2, Table 2.2 Comparative GDP per capita.
10  See Appendix 2, Table 2.2 Comparative GDP per capita.
11  See Appendix 3, Table 3.1 Comparative military expenditure.
12  For more information see Appendix 3, Table 3.1 Comparative military expenditure.
13  See Appendix 3, Table 3.1 Comparative military expenditure.
14  See Appendix 3, Table 3.2 Comparative military personnel.
15  See Appendix 3, Table 3.2 Comparative military personnel.
16  See Appendix 3, Table 3.2 Comparative military personnel.
17  For more information see Appendix 3, Table 3.2 Comparative military personnel.
18  This was directed by the USSR, who provided the Iraqis with the majority of its equipment and infrastructure (IISSe, 1974/75; IISSg, 1976/77; IISSh, 1977/78).
19  These demands came from all levels of society, and also sought to gain greater freedom through the liberalization and development programs undertaken by the Shah. For more information see Thurgood (1978: 5).
20  Branigin (1978: 8) makes note of the bandwagon effect following the religious movements. He suggests that the wealthy liberals dreamed of creating a Western style democracy and Marxist revolutionaries hoped for the institution of a proletariat.
21  Ayatollah Shariat-Madari had been, at that time, the foremost Islamic leader in Iran.
22  Branigin (1978: 8) also draws on the "carrot and stick" neo-liberalist policies the Shah attempted to diffuse the societal tension with.
23  Which happened when he finally left the country on January 16, 1979. For more information see Moseley (1979: 1); *Los Angeles Times* (1979a: 6); and Tuohy (1979: 1).

*Notes* 127

24 This treaty had provided the Iraqi regime with an important development partner at a time when many Western countries had not wanted to operate in Iraq as a result of the widespread nationalization that had occurred, particularly of the Iraqi Petroleum Company (*New York Times*, 1978a: 3).
25 With two members of the cabinet from the Iraqi Communist Party (*New York Times*, 1978a: 3).

## 5 The post-revolution period: phase 3 of Iran–Iraq relations

1 Indeed, this was increasingly evident in news reports in the post revolution period such as in McManus (1980: 10); Homan (1980: 18); Broder (1980: 10); Kifner (1980: 9); and *Washington Post* (1980: 17).
2 The Baathist regime viewed this revolution as dangerous due to its large Shi'ite community and the potential to export it to Iraq (IISS, 1980: 55–7). Reports emerged of more widespread persecution and the mass deportation undertaken by the Iraqis during 1979, where in one week alone the Iraqis were accused of deporting an estimated 30,000 Shi'ite Iraqis to the border with Iran (IISS, 1980: 49) expelled on the back of Iranian calls for Saddam Hussein to be overthrown.
3 See, for example, *Los Angeles Times* (1980a: 14); *Los Angeles Times* (1980b: 1); *Chicago Tribune* (1980: 13); and *Los Angeles Times* (1980c: 10).
4 These more conservative figures were published from the Charge D'Affaires of the Permanent Mission of Iran to the United Nations, October 1, 1980. There was also wide-spread reports of this in the media such as in the *Wall Street Journal* (1980: 3); Randal (1980: 18); and *Los Angeles Times* (1980: 5).
5 For more details, see the formal letter from the Permanent Representative of Iraq to the United Nations, June 20, 1980.
6 See also Kifner (1980: 3); Homan (1980: 18); *Washington Post* (1980: 17); and McManus, (1980: 10).
7 See, for example, *Washington Post* (1980: 12); *Los Angeles Times* (1980e: 15); and *Los Angeles Times* (1980f: 16).
8 See, for example, *Washington Post* (1980: 20); *Los Angeles Times* (1980f: 16); Charge D'Affaires of the Permanent Mission of Iran to the United Nations, July 23, 1980; and Permanent Representative of Iraq to the United Nations, August 19, 1980.
9 According to Hiro (1989: 1) the both the direct and indirect damaged caused by hostilities is "an astronomical figure of $1,190 billion."
10 See Appendix 1, Table 1.1 Comparative total population.
11 For more information see Appendix 1, Table 1.1 Comparative total population.
12 See Appendix 1, Table 1.3 Comparative urban population.
13 See Appendix 1, Table 1.3 Comparative urban population.
14 For more information see Appendix 2, Table 2.1 Comparative GDP. Iran nonetheless maintained a broad measure of superiority, with an advantage of 2.3:1.
15 See Appendix 2, Table 2.2 Comparative GDP per capita.
16 For more information regarding these figures see Appendix 2, Table 2.2 Comparative GDP per capita.
17 See Appendix 2, Table 2.2 Comparative GDP per capita.
18 For more information see Appendix 3, Table 3.1 Comparative military expenditure.
19 See Appendix 3, Table 3.1 Comparative military expenditure.
20 See Appendix 3, Table 3.2 Comparative military personnel.
21 For more information see Appendix 3, Table 3.2 Comparative military personnel.

22 Both IISS (1979) and Geller and Singer (1998) make note of this important withdrawal of American support following the hostage crisis
23 For more information regarding the expansion of the Iraqi armed forces see IISSh (1978/79); and IISSi (1979/80).
24 The IISS (1979: 42) makes note of this process, arguing that the removal of the political control and military monopoly under the Shah created a vacuum for the "fissiparous trend towards the reassertion of local nationalism and particularistic loyalties among Iran's many minorities." The revolutionary government had inherited a system of competing authorities, with its writ limited to a few major cities, including Tehran and Isfahan.
25 House and Bacon (1979: 1) argued that these movements were the immediate problem facing the revolutionary government following the removal of the Shah. It was thought at the time that the ability of Khomeini to build a functioning government in the face of these internal obstacles was a formidable task with slim chance of success (House and Bacon, 1979: 1). The IISS (1979: 43) also notes that resistance to the revolutionary government was felt among smaller minorities such as the Sunni and Baluchis.
26 See, for further documentation of this unrest, *Guardian* (1979b: 6); and *Guardian* (1979a: 5).

# Bibliography

## Primary sources

### *Newspapers*

Adams Schmidt, D., "Iraq Recognizes Kurdish Autonomy," *New York Times*, March 12, 1970: 8.
——, "Rulers of Iraq Place Priority On Consolidating Their Power," *New York Times*, March 13, 1970: 3.
——, "Shah's Martial Law Can't Stop Violence," *Observer*, September 10, 1978: 8.
——, "Iran Confronts Separatism Among Tribal Minorities," *Washington Post*, February 21, 1979: 10.
——, "Iranian Kurds Say Army Has Joined Drive Against Them," *Washington Post*, April 26, 1979: 29.
——, "Iran Charges New Iraqi Air Raid, Renews Bahrain," *Washington Post*, June 16, 1979: 18.
——, "Bani-Sadr Warns Iraq Not to Invade," *Washington Post*, April 12, 1980: 1.
Broder, J., "Oil is 'Open Sesame' Baghdad," *Chicago Tribune*, December 22, 1979: 11.
——, "Shi'ite vs. Sunni Splits Dim Mideast Peace Hopes," *Chicago Tribune*, April 19, 1980: 10.
Caputo, P., "The Iran-Iraq Border–Another Fuse Gets Short," *Chicago Tribune*, February 14, 1974: 3.
*Chicago Tribune*, "Iraq Arrests, Executes 29 in Coup Attempt," January 22, 1970: 18.
——, "Iraq Forces Quell Tribal Violence," July 13, 1972: 16.
——, "2 Killed in Clash of Iraq, Iran troops," January 3, 1973: 2.
——, "After Border Clash—Iraq, Iran Troop Buildup Reported," February 12, 1974: 4.
——, "U.N. to Take Up Iran-Iraq Feud," February 15, 1974: 15.
——, "56 Iraqis Die on Iran Border," March 7, 1974: 9.
——, "Iraq, Iran Find Stiff Oil Hikes Chase Buyers," January 17, 1977: 4.
——, "Report Iraq Executes 14," May 27, 1978: 8.
——, "Rage of Centuries Boils Among Iran's Desperate Arabs," June 10, 1979: 4.
——, "Iran Accuses Iraq of Border Attack," June 16, 1979: 8.

## Bibliography

———, "Is Iran Exporting Revolution?," October 8, 1979: 22.
———, "Dispute Worsens," April 10, 1980: 13.
Claiborne, W., "Bell Helicopter Starts Evacuating Key Employees From Iran," *Washington Post*, February 9, 1979: 19.
Clarity, J.F., "Iraqi Forces Seize Most Kurdish Towns," *New York Times*, September 27, 1974: 4.
———, "Iran's Help to Kurds Fighting Iraq Includes Arms, Secret Agents and Public Relations," *New York Times*, October 11, 1974: 12.
*Christian Science Monitor*, "Pressures on the Persian Gulf," February 9, 1970: 16.
Cockburn, P., "Land of Mystery and Prosperity," *The Times*, February 18, 1977: 6.
Cody, E., "Iraqis Must Learn to Read and Write – Or Else!," *Washington Post*, September 27, 1979: 26.
Cooley, J.K., "Iraq Accuses Iran and U.S. of Plot," *Christian Science Monitor*, January 24, 1970: 2.
———, "Leadership Shuffle in Iraq Signals New Internal Ferment," *Christian Science Monitor*, October 2, 1971: 14.
———, "Relations Between Iran, Iraq Tense," *Washington Post*, January 28, 1972: 21.
———, "Shah Outlines Iran's Position in Middle East," *Christian Science Monitor*, January 27, 1976: 6.
———, "Iraq Takes Moscow to Task," *Christian Science Monitor*, June 13, 1978: 4.
Cumming-Bruce, N., "Iranian Students Take Over US Embassy," *Guardian*, November 3, 1979: 1.
*Daily Star* (Beirut, Lebanon), July 28, 1971a: 3.
———, "Iraq Urges Arabs to Policy Reversal Relations with Iran, Britain," December 7, 1971b: 1.
———, "Iran Launches Campaign Against Iraq's Actions," January 5, 1972a: 3.
———, January 6, 1972b: 3.
———, "Iran See No Ties Between Gulf Issue, Iraqi Measures," January 11, 1972c: 1.
———, "Soviet, Iraqi Treaty Goes Into Effect," July 21, 1972d: 1.
———, "Military Aid to Iraq Under Study," September 16, 1972e: 1.
———, "Iraqi, Iranian Forces Clash," February 11, 1974a: 1.
———, "Iraqis, Iranians Reinforcing Borders after Heavy Clashes," February 12, 1974b: 1.
———, "Iran, Iraq Sign Accord Settling Long-Standing Border Differences," March 18, 1974c: 1.
———, November 11, 1974d: 6.
———, "Iraq, Iran End Dispute," March 7, 1975a: 2.
———, "Shah Says Dispute with Iraq Is Finally Over," March 8, 1975b: 2.
———, "Kurdish Stand toward Iraq-Iran Accord," March 9, 1975c: 2.
———, "Iraqi Amnesty Offer Prompts Kurdish Rebels to Surrender," March 15, 1975d: 2.
———, "KRP Backs Iraqi Govt. Against Rebels," March 17, 1975e: 2.
———, March 18, 1975f: 1.
———, "Military Power to Protect Iran's Wealth," March 18, 1975g: 2.
———, "Kurdish Rebellion Collapse: The War is Over, Barzani Says," March 23, 1975h: 2.
———, November 11, 1979: 11.

Davison, P., "Khomeini Envoys Again Try for Kurdish Peace," *Guardian*, March 22, 1979: 9.

De Onis, J., "Modernizing Iran Seeks Dominant Role in Region," *New York Times*, July 4, 1973: 3.

Durdin, T., "Iranian Anger in Border Issue Grows," *New York Times*, May 19, 1969: 2.

*Financial Times*, "Iranian Forces Fight On Against Oman Rebels," December 13, 1974: 8.

———, August 1, 1979: 2.

———, December 8, 1979: 2.

Fitchett, J., "Kurds Seize Area Along Iraq Border," *Washington Post*, March 19, 1974: 1.

Freed, K., "'Stable Chaos' in Iran; Rush to Leave Continues", *Los Angeles Times*, February 8, 1979: 12.

———, "Fighting Erupts in Southwest Iran as Arab Minority Pushes for Increased Autonomy," *Los Angeles Times*, May 31, 1979: 7.

Friendly, A., "Shah Arming Iran as Buffer Against Radical Arab States," *Washington Post*, June 7, 1969: 15.

———, "Shah's Reforms Attract Even Iranian Dissidents," *Washington Post*, June 15, 1969: 16.

*Guardian*, July 18, 1979a: 5.

———, July 21, 1979b: 6.

———, July 30, 1979c: 5.

———, November 13, 1979d: 6.

———, May 1, 1980: 6.

Godsell, G., "Shah Tells Why He Made Peace With Iraq," *Christian Science Monitor*, May 7, 1975: 3.

Henderson, S., "Iranians Admit Industry Hurt," *Financial Times*, January 8, 1980: 3.

Hijazi, I., "Iraq Wants to Revive Eastern Front," *Financial Times*, June 1, 1977: 7.

Hijazlln, I., "Iraq, The East Is a Little Less Red," *New York Times*, July 2, 1978: 4.

Hirst, D., "Iraq's War in the Kurdish Mountains," *Washington Post*, October 20, 1974: 5.

———, "Iraq's New Leader Faces Triple Challenge", *Guardian*, July 18, 1979: 5.

———, "'Plotters' arrested in Iraq's New Reign of Terror," Guardian, July 30, 1979: 1.

Hoagland, J., "Mistrust Imperils Iraqi-Kurdish Accord," *Washington Post*, July 12, 1972: 8.

———, "Kuwait Questions Arab Policy," *Washington Post*, March 31, 1973: 1.

———, "Boom Times in the Gulf," *Washington Post*, July 22, 1973: 1.

———, "Iranian Missiles Aid Kurds Against Iraq," *Washington Post*, November 15, 1974: 21.

———, "Iraq Tries to Boost Gulf Security," *Washington Post*, April 25, 1975: 16.

Homan, R., "Iran, Iraq on War Footing; Khomeini Urges Coup," *Washington Post*, April 9, 1980: 18.

House, K. and Bacon, K., "Iranian Outlook," *Wall Street Journal*, December 4, 1979: 1.

Housego, D., "Shah Strikes Blow at Iran's Political Life," *Financial Times*, January 3, 1975: 4.

## 132  Bibliography

Howe, M., "Iraqi Regime Gaining Self-Confidence," *New York Times*, December 25, 1971: 2.

———, "Iraq's Deportees: Pawns in a Power Game," *New York Times*, January 31, 1972: 6.

———, "New Anti-Communist Actions Were Reported–and Denied–Last Week," *New York Times*, January 7, 1979: 2.

———, "Iraq Discounts Religious Element in Iran Uprising," *New York Times*, February 26, 1979: 11.

Ibrahim, Y.M., "Iranian Oil Pipeline Is Cut, Reportedly by Arab Group," *New York Times*, July 12, 1979: 3.

———, "Inside Iran's Cultural Revolution," *New York Times*, October 14, 1979: 9.

Izzard, R., "UK Military Withdrawal Will Leave Iran as Strongest Power," *The Times*, December 16, 1970: 4.

Kifner, J., "Arabs Voicing Fear About Persian Gulf," *New York Times*, October 20, 1979: 3.

———, "Iran Moving Troops Against Kurds To Curb Unrest Over New Charter," *New York Times*, December 7, 1979: 1.

———, "Iraq's President Seeks to Become the New Tito," *New York Times*, June 22, 1980: 3.

Kifner, J., "Iraqis and Iranians Hurl Sharp Insults," *New York Times*, June 26, 1980: 9.

Kraft, J., "Detente in the Persian Gulf," *Washington Post*, April 13, 1975: 39.

———, "Iraq: Fending Off Ferment," *Washington Post*, April 24, 1979: 1.

Kutschera, C., "Baghdad Relies on Soviet Bloc for Armament," *Daily Star*, July 29, 1971: 3.

Lamb, D., "Yanks in Iran: No Place to Go but Home," *Los Angeles Times*, June 29, 1979: 1.

Lamb, D., "Iran's Foreign Policy Adrift in Sea of Isolation, Distrust," *Los Angeles Times*, June 24, 1979: 1.

Lewis Jr, J. W., "Iraq Says War With Kurds Is Settled," *Washington Post*, March 12, 1970: 32.

Lewis, F., "Iraq, Iran and Saudis Discussing Alliance," *New York Times*, June 18, 1978: 1.

Lippman, T.W., "Strike Closes Airport, Slowing Iranian Exodus," *Washington Post*, January 2, 1979: 16.

———, "Iraq Sees Neighboring Iran's Turmoil as Threat," *Washington Post*, April 11, 1979: 20.

*Los Angeles Times*, "Iran, Iraq Mass Troops in Water Rights Dispute," April 22, 1969: 15.

———, "Iraq Reports Making Peace With Rebel Kurds," March 12, 1970: 19.

———, "Iraq, Iran Clashing," March 4, 1974a: 2.

———, "Iraq and Iran Reported in Shelling Duel," March 5, 1974b: 2.

———, "Iraq and Iran Clash Anew," March 6, 1974c: 11.

———, "Iran-Iraq Border Battle in 3rd Day," March 7, 1974d: 6.

———, "Hundreds of Iraqis Killed, Kurds Claim," April 1, 1974e: 4.

———, "Treaty Ends Iran-Iraq Disputes," June 15, 1975: 2.

———, "Iran Recalls Envoys to Seven Arab States," January 8, 1976: 4.

———, "Iraq Reports Executing 21 Reds, Denies Soviet Policy Reversal," June 7, 1978: 1.

———, "Farewell to the Shah," January 17, 1979a: 6.

———, "Iran's Violent, Uncertain Road," April 20, 1979b: 6.

———, "Arab Minority in Iran Protests Treatment," April 28, 1979c: 14.

———, "24 Killed as Kurds Battle Iran Guards," July 15, 1979d: 9.

———, "Loss of Rights Causes Iranian Middle Class to Flee, Paper Says," September 16, 1979e: 11.

———, "Iran Army on Alert Against Iraq After Attack on Oil Facilities," April 8, 1980a: 14.

———, "Iran-Iraq Air Battle," April 9, 1980b: 1.

———, "Iranian Phantom Jet, 3 Helicopters Clash with Iraqi Choppers, Tehran TV Reports," April 10, 1980c: 10.

———, "Iraq Deports 5,700 Iranians", April 11, 1980d: 5.

———, "Iraq Reports 3rd Major Border Clash with Iran," June 30, 1980e: 15.

———, "Iraq Accuses Iran of Attack," July 29, 1980f: 16.

———, "Iraq Drops Iran Pact," September 17, 1980g: 1.

Marks, L., "Shah Puts Carter's Principles to the Test," *Observer*, November 20, 1977: 1.

Marr, P., "Coup Attempt Questioned: Iraqi Regime Faltering?," *Christian Science Monitor*, March 3, 1970: 3.

Martin, P., "Iran Forces on Full Alert in Dispute with Iraq," *The Times*, April 21, 1969: 4.

———, "Iraq: Eyes on the Gulf," *The Times*, April 3, 1970: 5.

McManus, D., "Jobless Take to Streets," *Los Angeles Times*, April 16, 1979: 1.

———, "Iran and Iraq Escalate War of Words," *Los Angeles Times*, April 3, 1980: 10.

Mehrawari, A., "Iran accelerating Major build-up of Armed, Naval Forces in Gulf," *Daily Star*, March 8, 1973: 2.

Melloan, G., "The Renaissance of Modern Iran," *Wall Street Journal*, May 8, 1973: 26.

Morris, J., "Our Problem Is Management, Iraqi Says," *Los Angeles Times*, January 3, 1977: 18.

Morris Jr, J.A., "Iran Water Resources Will Be Nationalized," *Los Angeles Times*, February 27, 1967: 4.

———, "Iran and Iraq Reach Accord on Settling Border Disputes," *Los Angeles Times*, March 7, 1975: 1.

———, "Territorial Squabbles Over Islands, Oil Trouble Iraq, Kuwait," *Washington Post*, December 26, 1976: 46.

Moseley, R., "Teary-Eyed Shah Flies Out of Iran and Millions Take to Streets in Joy," *Chicago Tribune*, January 17, 1979: 1.

*New York Times*, "Iranian Ship Sails on Disputed River," April 23, 1969a: 10.

———, "Iran Warns U.N. Tension Is Rising on Iraq Border," May 10, 1969b: 10.

———, "Iraq Reports Clash with Iran's Troops and Capture of 14," September 15, 1969c: 13.

———, "Amnesty for Kurds reported in Iraq," January 26, 1970a: 8.

## Bibliography

——, "5 Kurds Appointed to Iraqi Cabinet," March 30, 1970b: 5.
——, "Baghdad Presses Gulf-Area Issue," April 26, 1970b: 8.
——, "Reforms in Iran bring new hope," July 17, 1970c: 9.
——, "Arab Pact in Gulf Proposed by Iraq," July 19, 1970d: 11.
——, "Kurds Fighting in Iraq," January 16, 1972a: 44.
——, "Soviet and Iraq in 15-Year Pact," April 10, 1972b: 3.
——, "Border Troubles Reflect Iran-Iraq Power Struggle," May 14, 1972c: 3.
——, "30 Reported Killed in Iraqi-Kurd Clash," July 13, 1972d: 12.
——, "Iraq and Kuwait Clash at Border," March 21, 1973: 6.
——, "Iraq and Iran Exchange Charges in U.N. Council," February 21, 1974a: 8.
——, "Iran Puts Iraqi Dead at Over 50 in 3 Days of Fighting," March 7, 1974b: 3.
——, "Four Iraqis Killed in New Iran Fighting," March 8, 1974c: 8.
——, "Iraq and Iran Sign Accord To Settle Border Conflicts," March 7, 1975a: 1.
——, "Iraqi-Iranian Accord Signed," June 14, 1975b: 10.
——, "Iraq and Iran Sign Accords On Border and Other Issues," December 27, 1975c: 2.
——, "Carter Lauds Shah on His Leadership," November 16, 1977: 12.
——, "Iraq Said to Execute 14 as Strain With Reds Grows," May 27, 1978a: 3.
——, "Empress Pays Visit to Iraq," November 19, 1978b: 21.
——, "Iran is Said to Crush Kurd Revolt; Khomeini Bypasses Army Leaders," August 19, 1979a: 1.
——, "The Kurds Dig In; So Does Khomeini," September 2, 1979b: 1.
——, "Iraq Expels Iranian Ambassador," March 10, 1980a: 9.
——, "Iraq and Iran Report Border Clash," March 30, 1980b: 12.
——, "Iran and Iraq Press the War of Words," April 9, 1980c: 14.
——, "Iraq Ends 1975 Border Pact With Iran as Frontier Clashes Continue," September 18, 1980d: 8.
*Observer*, "Iraq: Still a Land of Middle-Eastern Promise," July 8, 1973: 6.
——, "The Arming of the Oil Kings," August 5, 1973.
——, "Shah's martial law can't stop violence", September 10, 1978: 8.
——, February 18, 1979: 8.
Ottaway, D. B., "Iran Seeks to Control Persian Gulf Entry," *Washington Post*, March 23, 1973: 1.
Pace, E., "Iran and Iraq Weigh a Persian Gulf Defense Pact," *New York Times*, May 11, 1975a: 2.
——, "Iran Assuming Britain's Former Role as Guardian of Persian Gulf States," *New York Times*, May 7, 1975b: 2.
——, "Iran Fights Rising Food Deficit," *New York Times*, May 21, 1975c: 2.
——, "Persian Gulf States Seeking Closer Ties," *New York Times*, June 10, 1975d: 3.
——, "Iran Backs Friendship Pact With Iraq," *New York Times*, May 16, 1976: 12.
——, "Exodus from Iran Growing as Troops Take Over Airport," *New York Times*, January 3, 1979: 1.
Pranay B.G., "War in a Key Northwest Iranian City: Iraq Buzzes It and Sometimes Bombs It," *New York Times*, October 9, 1980: 16.

Randal, J.C., "Shah's Economic Projects Hit Snags, Periling His Regime," *Washington Post*, April 2, 1978: 22.
——, "Shah's Foes Visit Dissident in France," *Washington Post*, October 16, 1978: 18.
——, "Slow Recovery Seen for Iran's Army," *Washington Post*, February 25, 1979: 1.
——, "Kurds' Autonomy Cries Rekindle Ethnic Flashpoint in Iran," *Washington Post*, March 2, 1979: 13.
——, "Iraq Moves to Sever 1975 Border Accord With Iran," *Washington Post*, November 1, 1979: 29.
——, "Iran's Military: Hard Hit By Revolutionary Chaos," *Washington Post*, December 9, 1979: 14.
——, "Iraq Expelling 20,000 Iranians Following Border Clashes," *Washington Post*, April 11, 1980: 18.
Roberts, G., "How the Shah Left the Kurds In the Lurch", *Observer*, March 30 30, 1975: 6.
Rosenthal, A.M., "On My Mind; The Soviet-Iraq Axis," *New York Times*, February 19, 1991: 17.
Schanche, D.A. and Tuohy, W., "Foreigners Seek to Leave Strife in Iran," *Los Angeles Times*, January 6, 1979: 11.
Scott-Plummer, S., "Ten-Year Battle for Gateway to the Gulf," *The Times*, April 19, 1973: 14.
Seale, P., "Shah Pledges 'Free' Election," *Observer*, August 13, 1978: 4.
Spanier, D., "Midas with a Military Touch Brings Power to Iran," *The Times*, December 13, 1972: 14.
Szulc, T., "U.S., Britain Quietly Back Military Build-Up of Iran," *New York Times*, July 25, 1971: 1.
Temko, N., "Baghdad Pushes Iraqis Toward Literacy, Progress," *Christian Science Monitor*, April 12, 1979: 4.
——, "New Trouble for Iran as Iraq Threatens its Western Border," *Christian Science Monitor*, April 8, 1980: 6.
*Times, The*, "Iran's Educational Revolution," September 25, 1971: 8.
——, "55 Killed and 81 Hurt in Fighting on Iran-Iraq Frontier," February 12, 1974.
——, "Kurds Left in the Lurch," March 11, 1975: 17.
——, "Growing Pains in Iran," January 5, 1977: 13.
*Wall Street Journal*, "Civilian Government takes over in Iran; Protests continue; Shah Clings to Throne," January 8, 1979: 7.
——, "Armies of Iraq and Iran Go On Alert as Baghdad Expels 7,000 Iranians," April 8, 1980: 3.
*Washington Post*, "Iran Strengthens Forces Along Iraq River Border," April 20, 1969: 16.
——, "Iraq Claims Incursion by Iranians," September 15, 1969: 10.
——, "Iraq, Soviets Sign Friendship Treaty," April 10, 1972: 14.
——, "Radio Baghdad Says Iraqi Forces Fought Iranian Troops Near Border," April 15, 1972: 13.
——, "Kurds Rap Ruling Party In Iraq," November 10, 1972: 22.
——, "Iran-Iraq Clash," January 15, 1973: 18.
——, "Iraq-Iran Clash," February 17, 1974: 19.

## 136  Bibliography

——, "Iraq Ousts 5 Kurds In Cabinet," April 9, 1974: 16.
——, "Iraq Accuses U.S. of Arming Rebellious Kurds," April 11, 1974: 15.
——, "Iran's Continuing Revolution," March 4, 1979: 6.
——, "Kurds Continue Attacks in Iranian Provincial City," March 22, 1979: 23.
——, "Jobless Iranians Stage Angry Protest," October 3, 1979: 10.
——, "Iraqi Jets, Tanks Reportedly Attack Iranian Border Town," May 31, 1980: 12.
——, "Iraqi President Accuses Iran of Racist, Expansionist Stand," July 18, 1980: 20.
——, "Khomeini Urges Moslems to Rise Against Corrupt," August 10, 1980: 17.
Thurgood, L., "Shah and Moslem Leaders Clash in Rising Chorus of Dissent," *Guardian*, January 17, 1978: 6.
——, "Tehran Paradox – Security Crackdown for Freedom," *Guardian*, September 26, 1978: 5.
——, "Night Arrests End Iran Bomb Attacks," *Guardian*, July 18, 1979: 5.
——, "Iran's Middle Classes Fear Their Future Under Islam," *Guardian*, September 20, 1979: 7.
Tuohy, W., "Oil-Rich Iran Bursting at Seams With Development," *Los Angeles Times*, March 23, 1975: 1, 7, and 8.
——, "Ill-Fated Dynasty," *Los Angeles Times*, January 17, 1979: 1.
Vakil, F., "Past, Present and Future," *New York Times*, January 25, 1976: 142.
Vicker, R., "Iran Flexes Its Muscles," *Wall Street Journal*, July 23, 1975: 14.
Vis Raein, P., "Iran Celebrates 10th Anniversary of Social Reform," *Daily Star*, January 23, 1973: 3.
Walz, J., "Iran's Shah Leads a White Revolution," *New York Times*, October 27, 1963: 210.
Weinraub, B., "Iran Irks Arabs but Keeps Israeli Ties," *New York Times*, December 30, 1973: 2.
Whitley, A. and McDermott, A., "Iran to Revise Military Deals," *Financial Times*, January 9, 1979: 4.
Winder, D., "U.N. Puts Out Long-Smouldering Iran-Iraq Border Dispute," *Christian Science Monitor*, June 5, 1974: 3.

## *Policy documents*

Letter dated February 12, 1974 from the Deputy Permanent Representative of Iraq to the United Nations addressed to the President of the Security Council. Available through the United Nations Bibliographic Information System: http://unbisnet.un.org:8080/ipac20/ipac.jsp?session=1WH1681128S37.96248&profile=bib&menu=search&submenu=subtab124&ts=1281681633185

Letter dated March 6, 1974 from the Permanent Representative of Iran to the United Nations addressed to the President of the Security Council. Available through the United Nations Bibliographic Information System: http://unbisnet.un.org:8080/ipac20/ipac.jsp?session=1WH1681128S37.96248&profile=bib&menu=search&submenu=subtab124&ts=1281681633185

Letter dated September 4, 1974 from the Permanent Representative of Iraq to the United Nations addressed to the President of the Security Council. Available

through the United Nations Bibliographic Information System: http://unbisnet. un.org:8080/ipac20/ipac.jsp?session=1WH1681128S37.96248&profile=bib&menu=search&submenu=subtab124&ts=1281681633185
Letter dated September 11, 1974 from the Permanent Representative of Iran to the United Nations addressed to the President of the Security Council. Available through the United Nations Bibliographic Information System: http://unbisnet.un.org:8080/ipac20/ipac.jsp?session=1WH1681128S37.96248&profile=bib&menu=search&submenu=subtab124&ts=1281681633185
Letter dated December 18, 1974 from the Permanent Representative of Iraq to the United Nations addressed to the President of the Security Council.
Letter dated April 29, 1980 from the Permanent Representative of Iraq to the United Nations addressed to the Secretary-General. Available through the United Nations Bibliographic Information System: http://unbisnet.un.org:8080/ipac20/ipac.jsp?session=1WH1681128S37.96248&profile=bib&menu=search&submenu=subtab124&ts=1281681633185
Letter dated June 20, 1980 from the Permanent Representative of Iraq to the United Nations addressed to the Secretary-General. Available through the United Nations Bibliographic Information System: http://unbisnet.un.org:8080/ipac20/ipac.jsp?session=1WH1681128S37.96248&profile=bib&menu=search&submenu=subtab124&ts=1281681633185
Letter dated October 1, 1980 from the Charge D'Affaires of the Permanent Mission of Iran to the United Nations addressed to the Secretary General. Available through the United Nations Bibliographic Information System: http://unbisnet.un.org:8080/ipac20/ipac.jsp?session=1WH1681128S37.96248&profile=bib&menu=search&submenu=subtab124&ts=1281681633185
2250th United Nations Security Council Meeting Held in New York on Wednesday October 15, 1980, at 3:30 p.m. Available through the United Nations Bibliographic Information System: http://unbisnet.un.org:8080/ipac20/ipac.jsp?session=1WH1681128S37.96248&profile=bib&menu=search&submenu=subtab124&ts=1281681633185

## *Reports*

Federation of American Scientists (a), T-62 Tank, accessed October 19, 2006: http://www.fas.org/man/dod-101/sys/land/row/t62tank.htm

—— (b), Chieftain Tank, accessed on October 19, 2006: http://www.fas.org/man/dod-101/sys/land/row/chieftain.htm

—— (c), MiG-21, accessed October 19, 2006: http://www.fas.org/man/dod-101/sys/ac/row/mig-21.htm

—— (d), MiG-23, accessed October 19, 2006: http://www.fas.org/nuke/guide/russia/airdef/mig-23.htm

—— (e), F-14, accessed October 19, 2006: http://www.fas.org/man/dod-101/sys/ac/f-14.htm

—— (f), T-54 Tank, accessed October 19, 2006: http://www.fas.org/man/dod-101/sys/land/row/t54tank.htm

International Institute for Strategic Studies (IISS) (1970), Strategic Studies, 1970, London; IISS.
—— (1971), Strategic Studies, London; IISS.
—— (1972), Strategic Studies, London; IISS.
—— (1973), Strategic Studies, London; IISS.
—— (1974), Strategic Studies, London; IISS.
—— (1975), Strategic Studies, London; IISS.
—— (1976), Strategic Studies, London; IISS.
—— (1977), Strategic Studies, London; IISS.
—— (1978), Strategic Studies, London; IISS.
—— (1979), Strategic Studies, London; IISS.
—— (1980), Strategic Studies, London; IISS.
—— (a) (1970/1971), The Military Balance, London; IISS.
—— (b) (1971/1972), The Military Balance, London; IISS.
—— (c) (1972/1973), The Military Balance, London; IISS.
—— (d) (1973/1974), The Military Balance, London; IISS.
—— (e) (1974/1975), The Military Balance, London; IISS.
—— (f) (1975/1976), The Military Balance, London; IISS.
—— (g) (1976/1977), The Military Balance, London; IISS.
—— (h) (1977/1978), The Military Balance, London; IISS.
—— (i) (1978/1979), The Military Balance, London; IISS.
—— (j) (1979/1980), The Military Balance, London; IISS.
United Nations Statistical Division, GDP Data, available through the United Nations Statistics Division, under the national accounts main aggregates database.

## Secondary sources

### Journal articles

Adeed, I. Dawisha, "Iraq: The West's Opportunity," *Foreign Policy*, No. 41 (Winter, 1980): 134–53.

Aghajanian, A., "Population Change in Iran, 1966–86: A Stalled Demographic Transition?" *Population Development Review*, Vol. 17, No. 4 (Dec., 1991): 703–15.

Andriole, S.J., Wilkenfeld, J., and Hopple, G.W., "A Framework for the Comparative Analysis of Foreign Policy Behavior," *International Studies Quarterly*, Vol. 19, No. 2 (Jun., 1975): 160–98.

As'ad, G., "Unilateral Withdrawal: A New Phase in Israel's Approach to the Palestinian Question," *Palestine-Israel Journal of Politics, Economics & Culture*, Vol. 13, No. 2 (2006): 35–41.

Ashton, N.J., "A Microcosm of Decline: British Loss of Nerve and Military Intervention in Jordan and Kuwait, 1958 and 1961," *Historical Journal*, Vol. 40, No. 4. (Dec., 1997): 1069–83.

Axelrod, R. and Keohane, R.O., "Achieving Cooperation under Anarchy: Strategies and Institutions," *World Politics*, Vol. 38, No. 1 (Oct., 1985): 227.

Ben-Yehuda, H. and Sandler, S., "Magnitude and Endurance in Interstate and Ethnic-State Crises: The Arab-Israeli Conflict, 1947–2000," *Journal of Peace Research*, Vol. 40, No. 3 (May, 2003): 271–85.

Blyth, M., "Structures Do Not Come with an Instruction Sheet: Interests, Ideas, and Progress in Political Science," *Perspectives on Politics*, Vol. 1, No. 4. (Dec., 2003): 695–706.

Bremer, S.A., "Dangerous Dyads: Conditions Affecting the Likelihood of Interstate War, 1816–1965," *Journal of Conflict Resolution*, Vol. 36, No. 2 (Jun., 1992): 309–41.

Brewer, T.L., "Issue and Context Variations in Foreign Policy: Effects on American Elite Behavior," *Journal of Conflict Resolution*, Vol. 17, No. 1 (Mar., 1973): 89–114.

Bueno de Mesquita, B., "Risk, Power Distributions, and the Likelihood of War," *International Studies Quarterly*, Vol. 25, No. 4 (Dec., 1981): 547.

Carlsnaes, W., "The Agency-Structure Problem in Foreign Policy Analysis," *International Studies Quarterly*, Vol. 36, No. 3. (Sep., 1992): 245–70.

Casetti, E., "Power Shifts and Economic Development: When Will China Overtake the USA?" *Journal of Peace Research*, Vol. 40, No. 6. (Nov., 2003): 661–75.

Chan, S., "Is There a Power Transition between the U.S. and China? The Different Faces of National Power," *Asian Survey*, Vol. 45, No. 5 (Sep./Oct., 2005): 688.

Claes, D.H., "The United States and Iraq: Making Sense of the Oil Factor," *Middle East Policy*, Vol. 12, No. 4 (Winter 2005): 48.

Clark, D.H. and Reed, W., "The Strategic Sources of Foreign Policy Substitution," *American Journal of Political Science*, Vol. 49, No. 3 (Jul., 2005): 609–24.

Colaresi, M., "When Doves Cry: International Rivalry, Unreciprocated Cooperation, and Leadership Turnover," *American Journal of Political Science*, Vol. 48, No. 3. (Jul., 2004): 555–70.

Colaresi, M.P. and Thompson, W.R., "Alliances, Arms Buildups and Recurrent Conflict: Testing a Steps-to-War Model," *Journal of Politics*, Vol. 67, No. 2 (May 2005): 345–64.

Cole, J., "A "Shiite Crescent"? The Regional Impact of the Iraq War," *Current History*. Vol. 105, Iss. 687 (Jan., 2006): 20.

Crescenzi, M.J.C. and Enterline, A.J., "Time Remembered: A Dynamic Model of Interstate Interaction," *International Studies Quarterly*, Vol. 45, No. 3 (Sep., 2001): 416.

Crescenzi, M.J.C., Enterline, A.J. and Long, S.B., "Bringing Cooperation Back In: A Fully Informed Dynamic Model of Interstate Interaction," *Conflict Management and Peace Science*, Vol. 25, No. 1 (2008): 264–80.

de Soysa, I., Oneal, J.R., and Park, Y., "Testing Power – Transition Theory Using Alternative Measures of National Capabilities," *Journal of Conflict Resolution*, Vol. 41, No. 4 (Aug., 1997): 509–28.

Deutsch, K.W. and Singer, J.D., "Multi Polar Power Systems and International Stability," *World Politics*, Vol. 16, No. 3 (Apr., 1964): 390–406.

DiCicco, J.M. and Levy, J.S. "Power Shifts and Problem Shifts: The Evolution of the Power Transition Research Program," *Journal of Conflict Resolution*, Vol. 43, No. 6 (Dec., 1999): 675–704.

# Bibliography

Diehl, P.F., "Arms Races to War: Testing Some Empirical Linkages," *Sociological Quarterly*, Vol. 26 (1985): 331–49.

——, "What Are They Fighting for? The Importance of Issues in International Conflict Research," *Journal of Peace Research*, Vol. 29, No. 3 (Aug., 1992): 333–44.

Djerejian, E.P., "From Conflict Management to Conflict Resolution," *Foreign Affairs*, Vol. 85, Iss. 6 (Nov./Dec., 2006): 41–8.

Doran, C.F., "Systemic Disequilibrium, Foreign Policy Role, and the Power Cycle: Challenges for Research Design," *Journal of Conflict Resolution*, Vol. 33, No. 3 (Sep., 1989): 371–401.

Druckman, D., "Social Exchange Theory: Premises and Prospects," *International Negotiation*, Vol. 3 (1998): 253–66.

Fettweis, C.J.A., "Revolution in International Relation Theory: Or, What If Mueller Is Right?" *International Studies Review*, Vol. 8, Iss. 4 (Dec., 2006): 677–97.

Fürtig, H., "Conflict and Cooperation in the Persian Gulf: The Interregional Order and US Policy," *Middle East Journal*, Vol. 61, Iss. 4 (Autumn 2007): 627–40.

Garnham, D., "Dyadic International War 1816–1965: The Role of Power Parity and Geographical Proximity," *Western Political Quarterly*, Vol. 29, No. 2 (Jun., 1976): 231–42

Geller, D.S., "Power Differentials and War in Rival Dyads," *International Studies Quarterly*, Vol. 37, No. 2 (Jun., 1993): 173–93.

Gibler, D.M., "Control the Issues, Control the Conflict: The Effects of Alliances that Settle Territorial Issues on Interstate Rivalries," *International Interactions*, Vol. 22, No. 4 (1997): 341–68.

Gochman, C.S. and Maoz, Z., "Militarized Interstate Disputes, 1816–1976: Procedures, Patterns and Insights," *Journal of Conflict Resolution*, Vol. 28, No.4 (Dec., 1984): 585–616.

Goertz, G. and Diehl, P.F., "The Initiation and Termination of Enduring Rivalries: The Impact of Political Shocks," *American Journal of Political Science*, Vol. 39 (1995): 30–52.

Goldmann, K. "Cooperation and Tension among Great Powers: A Research Note," *Cooperation and Conflict* Vol. 15 (1980): 31–45.

Goldmann, K., "Change and Stability in Foreign Policy: Détente as a Problem of Stabilization," *World Politics*, Vol. 34, No. 2 (Jan., 1982): 230–66.

Goldstein, J.S., "Great-Power Cooperation Under Conditions of Limited Reciprocity: From Empirical to Formal Analysis," *International Studies Quarterly*, Vol. 39 (1995): 453–77.

Goldstein, J.S. and Pevehouse, J.C., "Reciprocity, Bullying, and International Cooperation: Time-Series Analysis of the Bosnia Conflict," *American Political Science Review*, Vol. 91, No. 3. (Sep., 1997): 515–29.

Goldstein, J.S., Pevehouse, J.C., Gerner, D.J., and Telhami, S., "Reciprocity, Triangularity, and Cooperation in the Middle East, 1979–97," *Journal of Conflict Resolution*, Vol. 45, No. 5 (Oct., 2001): 593.

Gongora, T., "War Making and State Power in the Contemporary Middle East," *International Journal of Middle East Studies*, Vol. 29, No. 3 (Aug., 1997): 323–40.

# Bibliography 141

Harris, S., "China's Regional Policies: How Much Hegemony?" *Australian Journal of International Affairs*, Vol. 59, Iss. 4 (Dec., 2005): 481–92.

Hebron, L., James, P., and Rudy, M., "Testing Dynamic Theories of Conflict: Power Cycles, Power Transitions, Foreign Policy Crises and Militarized Interstate Disputes," *International Interactions*, Vol. 33, Iss. 1 (Jan.–Mar., 2007): 1–29.

Hensel, P.R., "Charting a Course to Conflict: Territorial Issues and Militarized Interstate Disputes, 1816–1992," *Conflict Management and Peace Science*, Vol. 15, No.1 (Spring, 1996): 43–73.

——, "An Evolutionary Approach to the Study of Interstate Rivalry," *Conflict Management and Peace Science*, Vol. 17, No. 2 (Fall, 1999): 179–206.

——, "Contentious Issues and World Politics: The Management of Territorial Claims in the Americas, 1816–1992," *International Studies Quarterly*, Vol. 45, No. 1 (Mar., 2001): 82;

Hensel, P.R., McLaughlin-Mitchell, S., Sowers, T.E., and Thyne, C.L., "Bones of Contention: Comparing Territorial, Maritime, and River Issues," *Journal of Conflict Resolution*, Vol. 52, Iss. 1 (Feb., 2008): 118.

Hopf, T., "The Promise of Constructivism in International Relations Theory," *International Security*, Vol. 23, No. 1. (Summer, 1998): 171–200.

Horowitz, S., "The Balance of Power: Formal Perfect and Practical Flaws," *Journal of Peace Research*, Vol. 38, No. 6 (Nov., 2001): 705–22.

Hudson, V.M. and Vore, C.S., "Foreign Policy Analysis Yesterday, Today, and Tomorrow," *Mershon International Studies Review*, Vol. 39, No. 2. (Oct., 1995): 209–38.

Hussein, S., "Development of the Iraqi-Iranian Dispute, 1847–1975," *Journal of Contemporary History*, Vol. 20, No. 3 (Jul., 1985): 483–92.

Jablonsky, D., "National Power," *Parameters*, Vol 27, Iss. 1 (Spring, 1997): 34–54.

Jervis, R., "Realism, Neoliberalism, and Cooperation: Understanding the Debate," *International Security*, Vol. 24, No. 1 (Summer, 1999): 42–63.

Juhasz, A., "Mission: Iraqi Oil," *Multinational Monitor*, Vol. 28, Iss. 1 (Jan./Feb., 2007): 30–4.

Kaldor, M., "Old Wars, Cold Wars, New Wars, and the War on Terror," *International Politics*, Vol. 42, Iss. 4 (Dec., 2005): 491.

——, "The 'New War' in Iraq," *Journal of Social & Political Theory*, Iss. 109, (Apr., 2006): 1–27.

Kang, D.C., "The Theoretical Roots of Hierarchy in International Relations," *Australian Journal of International Affairs*, Vol. 58, Iss. 3 (Sep., 2004): 337–52.

Kapisthalam, K., "Australia and Asia's Rise," *Australian Journal of International Affairs*, Vol. 60, Iss. 3 (Sep., 2006): 369–75.

Karsh, E., "Military Power and Foreign Policy Goals: The Iran–Iraq War Revisited," *International Affairs*, (Royal Institute of International Affairs) Vol. 64, No. 1 (Winter, 1987–8): 83–95.

Kelton, M., "Perspectives on Australian Foreign Policy, 2005," *Australian Journal of International Affairs*, Vol. 60, Iss. 2 (Jun., 2006): 229–46.

Keohane, R.O., "Reciprocity in International Relations", *International Organization*, Vol. 40, No. 1 (Winter, 1986): 1–27.

## Bibliography

Kinsella, D., "Nested Rivalries: Superpower Competition, Arms Transfers, and Regional Conflict", *International Interactions*, Vol. 15 (1995): 109–25.

Kober, A., "Does the Iraq War Reflect a Phase Change in Warfare?", *Defense & Security Analysis*, Vol. 21, Iss. 2 (Jun., 2005): 121–42.

Kreft, H., "Power Shifting," *The World Today*, Vol. 62, Iss. 8/9 (Aug./Sep., 2006).

Kuperman, R.D., "A Dynamic Framework for Analyzing Foreign Policy Decision Making," *International Studies Review*, No. 8 (2006), 537–54.

Lamborn, A.C., "Risk and Foreign Policy Choice," *International Studies Quarterly*, Vol. 29, No. 4 (Dec., 1985): 385–410.

Layne, C., "Who Lost Iraq and Why It Matters: The Case for Offshore Balancing," *World Policy*, Vol. 24, Iss. 3 (Fall 2007): 38–52.

Lebovic, J.H., "The Limits of Reciprocity: Tolerance Thresholds in Superpower Conflict," *Journal of Peace Research*, Vol. 40, No. 2. (Mar., 2003): 139–58.

Lee, D.S., "When Are Power Shifts Dangerous?: Military Strategy and Preventive War," *Journal of International and Area Studies*, Vol. 13, Iss. 2 (Dec., 2006): 53–71.

Leeds, B.A. and Davis, D.R., "Beneath the Surface: Regime Type and International Interaction," *Journal of Peace Research*, Vol. 36, No. 1 (Jan., 1999).

Lemke, D., "The Continuation of History: Power Transition Theory and the End of the Cold War," *Journal of Peace Research*, Vol. 34, No. 1 (Feb., 1997): 23–36.

Lemke D. and Werner, S., "Power Parity, Commitment to Change, and War," *International Studies Quarterly*, Vol. 40, No. 2 (Jun., 1996): 235–60.

Leng, R.J., "Reciprocating Influence Strategies in Interstate Crisis Bargaining," *Journal of Conflict Resolution*, Vol. 37, No. 1 (Mar., 1993): 3.

——, "Reciprocity in Recurring Crises", *International Negotiation*, Vol. 3 (1998): 197–226.

Levi, W., "Ideology, Interests and Foreign Policy," *International Studies Quarterly*, Vol. 14, No. 1 (Mar., 1970): 3.

Lieven, A., White, W., Katzman, K., and Lang, W.P., "Iraq, Iran, Israel and the Eclipse of U.S. Influence: What Role For America Now?" *Middle East Policy*, Vol. 14, Iss. 1 (Spring, 2007): 1–26.

McLaughlin-Mitchell, S. and Prins, B.C., "Beyond Territorial Contiguity: Issues at Stake in Democratic Militarized Interstate Disputes," *International Studies Quarterly*, Vol. 43, No. 1 (Mar., 1999): 169.

Mansbach, R. and Vasquez, J., "The Effect of Actor and Issue Classifications on the Analysis of Global Conflict-Cooperation," *Journal of Politics*, Vol. 43, No. 3, (Aug., 1981): 861–74.

Mearsheimer, J.J. and Walt, S.M., "An Unnecessary War", *Foreign Policy*, No. 134 (Jan., 2003): 50–9.

Miller, B., "The Global Sources of Regional Transitions from War to Peace," *Journal of Peace Research*, Vol. 38, No. 2 (Mar., 2001): 199–225.

Mintz, A., Geva, N., Redd, S.B., and Carnes, A., "The Effect of Dynamic and Static Choice Sets on Political Decision Making: An Analysis Using the Decision Board Platform," *American Political Science Review*, Vol. 91, No. 3. (Sep., 1997): 553–66.

Mofid, K., 'Economic Reconstruction of Iraq: Financing the Peace", *Third World Quarterly*, Vol. 12, Iss. 1 (Jan., 90): 48.

Moran, T.H., "Iranian Defense Expenditures and the Social Crisis", *International Security*, Vol. 3, No. 3 (Winter, 1978–9): 178–92.

Morse, E.L., "Fighting for Oil?" *National Interest*, No. 76 (Summer, 2004): 37–40.

Morton, J.S. and Starr, H., "Uncertainty, Change, and War: Power Fluctuations and War in the Modern Elite Power System," *Journal of Peace Research*, Vol. 38, No. 1 (Jan., 2001): 49–66.

Moul, W., "Power Parity, Preponderance, and War between Great Powers, 1816–1989," *Journal of Conflict Resolution*, Vol. 47, No. 4 (Aug., 2003): 468–89.

Neff, D., "The U.S., Iraq, Israel, and Iran: Backdrop to War," *Palestine Studies*, Vol. 20, No. 4 (Summer, 1991): 23–41.

Niou E.M.S. and Ordeshook, P.C., "A Theory of the Balance of Power in International Systems," *Conflict Resolution*, Vol. 30, No. 4 (Dec., 1986): 685–715.

Nofal, M., "The Centrality of the Palestinian-Israeli Conflict for Middle East Peace," *Palestine-Israel Journal of Politics, Economics & Culture*, Vol. 11, No. 1 (2004): 22–9.

Nye, Jr., J.S., "The Changing Nature of World Power," *Political Science Quarterly*, Vol. 105, No. 2 (Summer, 1990): 177–92.

Ozkececi-Taner, B., "Reviewing the literature on Sequential/Dynamic Foreign Policy Decision Making," *International Studies Review*, Vol. 8, No. 3 (Sep. 2006): 545–54.

Parasiliti, A.T., "The Causes and Timing of Iraq's Wars: A Power Cycle Assessment," *International Political Science Review/ Revue internationale de science politique*, Vol. 24, No. 1, Power Cycle Theory and Global Politics. Cycle de pouvoir et politique mondiale. (Jan., 2003): 151–65.

Parsi, T., "Israel-Iranian Relations Assessed: Strategic Competition from the Power Cycle Perspective," *Iranian Studies*, Vol. 38, Iss. 2 (Jun., 2005): 247–69.

Peou, S., "Realism and Constructivism in Southeast Asian Security Studies Today: A Review Essay," *Pacific Review*, Vol. 15, Iss. 1 (Feb., 2002): 119–39.

Petersen, K. "There is More to the Story than "Us-Versus-Them': Expanding the Study of Interstate Conflict and Regime Type Beyond a Dichotomy," *Peace Economics, Peace Science and Public Policy*, Volume 14, No. 1 (2008): 1–35.

Pouliot, V., "'Sobjectivism': Toward a Constructivist Methodology," *International Studies Quarterly*, Vol. 51, No. 2 (Jun., 2007): 59–384.

Qingguo, J., "Peaceful Development: China's Policy of Reassurance," *Australian Journal of International Affairs*, Vol. 59, No. 4 (Dec., 2005): 493–507.

Rajmaira, S., "Indo-Pakistani Relations: Reciprocity in Long-Term Perspective," *International Studies Quarterly*, Vol. 41, No. 3 (Sep., 1997): 547–60.

Ramazani, R.K., "Iran's Revolution: Patterns, Problems and Prospects," *International Affairs*, Vol. 56, No. 3 (Summer, 1980): 448.

Rarkin, D. and Thompson, W.R., "Power Transition, Challenge and the (Re)Emergence of China," *International Interactions*, Vol. 29, No. 4 (Oct.–Dec., 2003): 315–42.

Rasler, K., "Shocks, Expectancy Revision, and the De-escalation of Protracted Conflicts: The Israeli-Palestinian Case" *Journal of Peace Research*, Vol. 37, Iss. 6 (Nov., 2000): 699–721.

Razi, G.H., "An Alternative Paradigm to State Rationality in Foreign Policy: The Iran–Iraq War," *Western Political Quarterly*, Vol. 41 No. 4. (Dec., 1988): 689–723.

Reed, W., "Information, Power, and War," *American Political Science Review*, Vol. 97, No. 4 (Nov., 2003): 633–41.

Rendall, M., "Defensive Realism and the Concert of Europe," *Review of International Studies*, Vol. 32, No. 3, (Jul., 2006).

Renfrew, N.M., "Who Started the War?" *Foreign Policy*, No. 66 (Spring, 1987): 98–108.

Rosecrance, R., "Australia, China and the US," *Australian Journal of International Affairs*, Vol. 60, No. 3 (Sep., 2006): 364–68.

Schampel Jr, J.S., "Limits of American Power," *Political Science Quarterly*, Vol. 117, No. 4 (Winter, 2002/2003): 545

Schampel, J.H., "Change in Material Capabilities and the Onset of War: A Dyadic Approach," *International Studies Quarterly*, Vol. 37, No. 4 (Dec., 1993), 395–408.

Schweller, R.L., "New Realist Research on Alliances: Refining, Not Refuting, Waltz's Balancing Proposition," *American Political Science Review*, Vol. 91, No. 4 (Dec., 1997): 927.

Siverson, R.M. and Sullivan, M.P., "The Distribution of Power and the Onset of War," *Journal of Conflict Resolution*, Vol. 27, No. 3 (Sep., 1983): 474.

Skelly, J.M., "A Constructivist Approach to Peace Studies," *Peace Review*, Vol. 14, No. 1 (Mar., 2002): 57–60.

Slater, J., "Lost Opportunities for Peace in the Arab-Israeli Conflict: Israel and Syria, 1948–2001," *International Security*, Vol. 27, No. 1 (Summer, 2002): 79–106.

Snyder, J., "One World, Rival Theories," *Foreign Policy*, No. 145 (Nov./Dec., 2004): 52–62.

Stork, J., "Iraq and the War in the Gulf," *MERIP Reports*, No. 97 (Jun., 1981): 3–18.

Swearingen, W.D., "Geopolitical Origins of the Iran–Iraq War", *Geographical Review*, Vol. 78, No. 4. (Oct., 1988): 405–16.

Sweeney, K.J., "The Severity of Interstate Disputes: Are Dyadic Capability Preponderances Really More Pacific?" *Journal of Conflict Resolution*, Vol. 47, No. 6 (Dec., 2003): 728–50.

Thompson, W.R., "Polarity, the Long Cycle, and Global Power Warfare," *Conflict Resolution*, Vol. 30, No. 4 (Dec., 1986): 587–615.

Thompson, W.R., "Systemic Leadership, Evolutionary Processes, and International Relations Theory: The Unipolarity Question," *International Studies Review*, Vol. 8, No. 1 (Mar., 2006): 1–22.

Treverton, G. and Jones, S., "Measuring Power: How to Predict Future Balances," *Harvard International Review*, Vol. 27, No. 2 (Summer, 2005): 54–8.

Ukeles, J.B., "Policy Analysis: Myth or Reality?" *Public Administration Review*, Vol. 37, No. 3 (May–Jun., 1977): 223–8.

Vasquez, J.A., "The Tangibility of Issues and Global Conflict: A Test of Rosenau's Issue Area Typology," *Journal of Peace Research*, Vol. 20, No. 2 (Jun., 1983). 179–92.

Vasquez, J.A., "Why Do Neighbors Fight? Territoriality, Proximity, or Interactions," *Journal of Peace Research*, No. 32 (Aug., 1995): 277–93.

Vasquez, J.A., "Comparative Foreign Policy; Fad, Fantasy, or Field?" *International Studies Quarterly*, Vol. 12, No. 3 (Sep., 1968): 313.

Verrastro, F.A., Placke, J.A., and Hegburg, A.S., "Securing U.S. Energy in a Changing World," *Middle East Policy*, Vol. 11, No. 4 (Winter, 2004): 1–25.

Volgy, T.J. and Imwalle, L.E. "Hegemonic and Bipolar Perspectives on the New World Order," *American Journal of Political Science*, Vol. 39, No. 4 (Nov., 1995): 819–34.

Wallace, M., "Arms Races and Escalation: Some New Evidence," *Journal of Conflict Resolution*, Vol. 23 (1979): 3–16.

Ward, M., "Cooperation and Conflict in Foreign Policy Behavior: Reaction and Memory," *International Studies Quarterly*, Vol. 26, No. 1 (Mar., 1982): 94.

Ward, M.D. and Rajimaira, S., "Reciprocity and Norms in U.S.-Soviet Foreign Policy," *Journal of Conflict Resolution*, Vol. 36, No. 2 (Jun., 1992): 342–68.

Weede, E., "Overwhelming Preponderance as a Pacifying Condition among Contiguous Asian Dyads, 1950–1969," *Journal of Conflict Resolution*, Vol. 20, No. 3. (Sep., 1976): 395–411.

Weinstein, F.B., "The Uses of Foreign Policy in Indonesia: An Approach to the Analysis of Foreign Policy in the Less Developed Countries," *World Politics*, Vol. 24, No. 3 (Apr., 1972): 356–81.

Wenger, M. and Anderson, D., "The Gulf War," *MERIP Middle East Report*, No. 148, Re-Flagging the Gulf. (Sep.–Oct., 1987): 23–6.

Wohlforth, W., "Unipolar Stability," *Harvard International Review*, Vol. 29, No. 1 (Spring, 2007): 44–8.

Woosang, K., "Power Parity, Alliance, Dissatisfaction, and Wars in East Asia, 1860–1993," *Journal of Conflict Resolution*, Vol. 46, No. 5 (Oct., 2002): 654–71.

Zhu, Z., "Power Transition and U.S.-China Relations: Is War Inevitable?" *Journal of International and Area Studies*, Vol. 12, No. 1 (Jun., 2005): 1.

Zimmerman, W., "Issue Area and Foreign Policy Process: A Research Note in Search of a General Theory," *American Political Science Review*, Vol. 47, No. 4, (Dec., 1973): 1204–12.

## Books and articles

Abraham, H. Maslow (1970), *Motivation and Personality* (3rd edn.), New York: Harper Collins.

Axelrod, R.M. (1990), *The Evolution of Cooperation*, London: Penguin.

Claude, I.L. (1962), *Power and International Relations*, New York: Random House.

Palit, D.K. (1972), *The Lightning Campaign: The Indo-Pakistan War 1971*, Salisbury: Compton Press.

Dupuy, T.N. (1978), *Elusive Victory: The Arab-Israeli Wars, 1947–1974*, London: Macdonald and Jane's.

Duri, A.A. (1987), *The Historical Formation of the Arab Nation, A Study in Identity and Consciousness*, (trans. Lawrence I. Conrad), Croom Helm, New York.

Esherick, J.W., Pickowicz, P.G., and Walder, A.G. (eds) (2006), *The Chinese Cultural Revolution as History*, California: Stanford University Press.

Evan, Luard (1987), *War in International Society: A Study in International Sociology*, New Haven: Yale University Press.

## Bibliography

Harold, J. Lasswell and Abraham K. (1950), *Power and Society*, New Haven: Yale University Press.

Hiro, P. (1989), *The Longest War: The Iran-Iraq Military Conflict*. London: Grafton Books.

Hocking, B. and Smith, M. (1990), *World Politics: An Introduction to International Relations*, Great Britain: Harvester Wheatsheaf.

Jacob, B. and Richard J. (1997), *International Conflict: A Chronological Encyclopaedia of Conflicts and Their Management 1945–1995*, Washington DC: Congressional Quarterly Books.

John, V. (1993), *The War Puzzle*, New York: Cambridge University Press.

Kalevi, J.H. (1991), *Peace and War: Armed Conflicts and International Order, 1648–1989*, New York: Cambridge University Press.

Mawby, S. (2005), *British Policy in Aden and the Protectorates 1955–67: Last Outpost of a Middle East Empire*, New York: Routledge.

Organski, A.F.K. and Kugler, J. (1980), *The War Ledger*, Chicago: University of Chicago Press.

Organski, A.F.K. (1968), *World Politics*, (2nd edn), New York: Knopf, p. 294.

Palit, D.K. (1972), *The Lightning Campaign: The Indo-Pakistan War 1971*, Salisbury: Compton Press.

Paul, T.V., Wirtz, J.J., and Fortmann, M. (eds) (2004), *Balance of Power: Theory and Practice in the 21st Century*, California: Stanford University Press.

Pett, S. (ed.), *Lightning Out of Israel: The Six-Day War in the Middle East*, New York: Associated Press.

Plano, J.C. and Olton, R. (1982), *The International Relations Dictionary* (3rd edn), USA: ABC-Clio.

Porter, G. (2005), *Perils of Dominance: Imbalance of Power and the Road to War in Vietnam*, Berkeley: University of California Press.

Reus-Smit, C. (2004), *American Power and World Order*, Cambridge: Polity Press.

Richardson, L.F. (1960), *Arms and Insecurity*, Pittsburgh, PA: Boxwood Press.

Robinson, J. (1970), *The Cultural Revolution in China*, Harmondsworth, Penguin Books.

Rosenan, J.N. (1966), "Pre-Theories and Theories of Foreign Policy," in R.B. Farrell (ed.), *Approaches to Comparative and International Politics*, Evanston, IL: Northwestern University Press, pp. 27–93.

Rosenan, J.N. (1967), "Foreign Policy as An Issue," in James Rosenau (ed.), *Domestic Sources of Foreign Policy*, New York: Free Press, pp. 11–50.

Singer, J.D., Bremer, S., and Stuckey, J. (1972), "Capability Distribution, Uncertainty, and Major Power War, 1820–1965," in Bruce Russett (ed.) *Peace, War, and Numbers*, Beverly Hills: Sage, pp. 19–48.

Sisson, R. and Rose, L.E. (1990), *War and Secession: Pakistan, India, and the Creation of Bangladesh*, Berkeley: University of California Press.

Teiwes, F.C. and Sun, W. (1999), *China's Road to Disaster: Mao, Central Politicians, and Provincial Leaders in the Unfolding of the Great Leap Forward, 1955–1959*, New York: M.E. Sharpe.

Vasquez, J.A. and Elman, C. (2003), *Realism and the Balancing of Power: A New Debate*, New Jersey: Prentice Hall.

Waltz, K.N. (1979), *Theory of International Politics*, USA: Addison-Wesley.

Zaheer, H. (1994), *The Separation of East Pakistan: The Rise and Realization of Bengali Muslim Nationalism*, Karachi: Oxford University Press.

# Index

absorption 38, 57, 61, 78, 95
Abu Musa 51
acquiescence, demonstrated Iraqi 69
actors 11, 13–16, 19, 26–7, 29, 45, 107
advantage 57–8, 74–5, 77, 93, 95, 99
aggression, repel Iraqi 53
agreement 56, 70, 72, 78, 80, 83, 106
aircraft 62, 79, 95; transport/tanker 78–9
Algiers Agreement 6–7, 42, 56, 66, 68–70, 83–5, 89–90, 100, 104, 107
alliances 18
analysts 2, 34
approaches 4, 6, 8–9, 11–12, 22, 25, 29–30, 32, 35, 42, 44, 103–5, 110; integrated 1–44, 67–8, 103–5, 108; integrative 5–6, 10; issues-based 10–12, 24, 41; power-based 6; power preponderance 32; stimulus-response 25–6; traditional 2, 12–13
Arab community 47
Arab-Israeli conflicts 5, 39
Arab movements 98
Arab states 51, 54
Arab waterway 46, 69–70
Arabic-speaking minority in Iran 98
Arabs 5, 47–9, 54–5, 66, 71, 89, 97–8, 106
argument, balancing 31
armed forces 37–8, 49, 55, 63–4, 73, 79, 83, 90, 96–7, 100
army 61, 63, 79, 95–7
artillery 83
authority 42, 54, 63, 83, 88, 97–8, 104
autonomy: greater 63, 97, 101; increased 98

average: higher 57–8, 60; lifted Iraq's 60
Ayatollah 97–8
Ayatollah Khaghani 98
Ayatollah Khomeini 4–5, 69, 72–3, 86, 88, 90, 96–7, 100, 106, 108
Ayatollah Shariat-Madari 82, 97

Baathist government 88–9, 106
Baathist regime 43, 51–2, 54–5, 64, 69, 83–4, 89
backdrop 7, 68–9, 72–3, 105
Baghdad 48, 51–2, 59, 61, 63, 95
Bahrain 51, 88–9
Bakhtiar 73
balance 30–1, 33
balance of power 4, 6, 32–4
balance of power theory 31, 42
battle 53–4, 90
behavior 3–5, 11, 17, 21, 25–7, 29–30, 36, 40–1, 43, 45, 52–3, 56, 109; conflictual 17; power maximizing 13
behavior-begets-behavior 29
bilateral relations 27, 41–2, 53, 73, 101
border clashes 47–8, 53
border skirmishes 55–6, 90, 107
borders 7, 24, 47, 49–51, 53, 85, 90, 105; eastern 54–5; mutual 30, 48, 66
Bosnian conflict 28
Britain 36, 78–9
Broadening Iranian Power Preponderance 56

campaign 52, 54
capabilities 5, 16, 18, 32, 36–8, 61, 66, 72, 80, 101–2; material 1–2, 9; relative power 34, 56

*Index* 149

change 7, 19, 27–8, 33–4, 41, 45, 56, 88, 104; generating conflict 15
Chieftain Tanks 78, 95
cities 39, 52, 81
clashes, intermittent 63
Clear Iranian Superiority 63
clear superiority 57
commitment 17, 48
community, large Iranian expatriate 51
comparative power capabilities 7, 11, 33, 36, 45, 61, 105, 107–8
comparative power relationship 34
competition 19, 31, 33, 68–9
conditions, permissive 8, 85–6, 91
conflict 1–8, 10–22, 25, 27–8, 30, 33–5, 37, 39–45, 50, 54–6, 66–8, 85–6, 91, 101, 103, 105–9; border 70; cessation of 43, 68; dyadic 27; enduring 44; evolution of 12, 44, 103, 109; issues-based 17; initial 109; internal 63; issues-based explanations of 18, 25; militarized 18, 35; reciprocal 56; regional 28; sporadic violent 90; unfolding 53
Conflict and Peace Data Bank and World Event/Interaction Survey 2
conflict cycles 3, 55, 102, 107, 109; broader 66; clear escalatory 5; reciprocal 18, 66, 91
Conflict Escalation to War 101
conflict interaction 28
conflict outcomes 10
Conflict Spiral 66, 101
conflict spiral, potential 26
conflictual 8, 13–16, 18, 25, 27, 40, 42, 45, 104, 107–8; stimulated 84
conflictual behavior 17, 23
conflictual cycle 85
conflictual escalation 66
conflictual evolution 86
conflictual interaction 3, 7, 10, 17, 20, 30, 68, 86, 103
conflictual issue resolution 46
conflictual management techniques 18
conflictual relations 30
confrontation, total 97

contention 2–3, 5–9, 11–12, 14–25, 38–46, 48, 56, 66, 68, 85, 87, 90, 101, 103–8
control 16–17, 20–1, 33, 47, 49, 51, 54, 64–5, 69, 87, 96, 105
convergence 34, 45, 60–1, 75, 77, 81, 91–3, 102; rapid 7–8, 68, 94, 105, 108
cooperation 12–14, 19, 26–8, 41, 43, 62, 68, 71, 88, 101
Cooperative Cycle 84–5
Cooperative foreign policy reciprocity 68
counter Iranian influence 84

defection 26–7
defence 37, 47
demographic indicators 37–8, 56–9, 73–5, 91–3, 95, 99
demonstrations 88, 97, 99
Détente GDP 75–6
Détente Military Expenditure 76
Détente Military Personnel 77
détente period 42, 68–85, 105, 107
Détente Total Population 74
Détente Urban Population 74
diplomatic relations 43, 51, 68
disputes 11–12, 18–19, 21, 46
divergence 65–6, 77
Divergence and Iranian Superiority 60, 73
domestic industries 24, 37–8, 99
dyadic power distributions 7, 32
dyadic relationships 6, 9, 26–7, 30, 33–4, 41–2, 103, 109
dyads 4, 17–18, 26–8, 33, 35–6, 42
dynamic power capabilities 9, 45–6, 86, 91, 104, 109
Dynamic Power Distribution 56, 73, 91
dynamic variable 33

economic capabilities 36–7, 58–9, 75, 77, 92–3, 95
economy 38–9, 64, 81, 84, 99–100
emergence 16, 28, 33, 86–7, 106, 109
emissaries 88
environment 29, 34
equipment 78–9; new 79–80, 100
escalate conflict 66

escalating 10, 46, 90–1
escalation 6–8, 28, 30, 85, 105, 107; explaining conflict 3, 10; understanding conflict 3, 44, 108
escalation of conflict 3, 6, 8–10, 18, 22, 30, 41, 44, 85–6, 91, 101, 109
Escalatory and Reciprocal Conflict Spiral 88
escalatory conflict cycle 7–8, 41–2, 101, 105, 108
evolution 1, 3–5, 41–3, 46, 71, 86, 90, 103, 106, 108–9
examination of dynamic power capabilities 9, 86, 109
expectations 25, 39–42, 104–5
explanation 3, 5–9, 13, 34, 40, 44, 91, 103, 105–6; issues-based 3, 6, 8

F-4E 62
F-5E 62, 78
fighters, advanced 62
forces 38, 79–80, 89
foreign policy 10, 13–14, 73
foreign policy behavior 2–3, 5, 9–10, 12–18, 29, 44, 46; cooperative 2
foreign policy goals 4–5, 107
foreign policy interactions 1, 3, 5, 11, 13, 45–6, 84, 106; cooperative 84
foreign policy output analysis 29
foreign policy reciprocity (FPR) 8–9, 28, 30, 38–40, 44–6, 48, 67, 84–6, 102–4, 106–9
France 36, 78–80
freedom 13, 23, 65, 82

GDP (Gross Domestic Product) 38–9, 58–9, 75, 93
GDP Per Capita 38, 58, 75–6, 93
Germany 36, 79
government, provisional 96
groups 2, 14, 21–3, 29, 31, 47, 69, 81–2, 97–8
growth 41, 59–60, 62, 74, 76, 81, 92, 104; annual 60
Gulf region 46, 50–1, 53–4, 71, 84
Gulf security pact 50, 70
Gulf States 53, 70, 89

Hostile Reciprocity and Conflict Spiral 48

hostile relations 46, 90
hostilities 6, 35, 37, 43, 49, 56, 90, 106–7

ICP (Iraqi Communist Party) 47, 83, 100
ideology 15, 20
independence 8, 23, 97–8, 105–6
instability, domestic 7, 34, 66, 68, 72, 85, 107
installation 7, 43, 64, 82, 86, 88, 95–6, 108
instruments 2, 9, 16
Integrated Approach to Understanding Interstate Conflict Escalation 9
interactions 3–10, 17–18, 25–8, 30, 32, 40–2, 46, 69–71, 85–6, 104–7; bilateral 41, 56, 90, 102; cooperative 15, 73; dyadic 28
international interactions 10, 42
international relations 1, 25
interstate conflict 1, 10, 32, 108
interstate conflict escalation 6, 40
interstate interaction 2–4, 6–7, 9, 11, 17, 24–9, 41, 44–8, 66, 68, 70, 72, 84–5, 88, 104–6, 109
interstate relations 25, 106
Iran: characterized 5; entered 73; invade 4, 40; northwestern 72; plagued 96; portray 50; post-revolution 97; southwest 98; western 97
Iran–Iraq conflict 11, 38
Iran–Iraq Relations 44, 68, 71–2, 86
Iran–Iraq relationship 66
Iran–Iraq War 3–5, 7–11, 34, 39–41, 43–4, 85, 90, 103–4, 108–9
Iranian abrogation 42, 51, 56
Iranian accusation 89
Iranian advantage 60, 92
Iranian aggression 48
Iranian Air Force 95
Iranian ambassador to Iraq 89
Iranian and Iraqi border posts 71
Iranian and Iraqi expenditures 60
Iranian and Iraqi interstate interaction 105
Iranian and Iraqi power 95
Iranian and Iraqi relations 7, 11, 54
Iranian citizens 52; ejecting 30

Index 151

Iranian consulates 50
Iranian demands 69, 106
Iranian economy 99
Iranian emissaries 88
Iranian expansion 30
Iranian expansionism 90
Iranian expatriate colony 51
Iranian-flagged ships 49
Iranian forces 51, 55
Iranian government 52, 81, 87–8; revolutionary 7
Iranian influence 47
Iranian interaction, underlying 68
Iranian–Iraqi Friendship Treaty 71
Iranian–Iraqi interaction 69
Iranian Kurds 50
Iranian leadership 70
Iranian Lower House of Parliament 52
Iranian military 78, 83
Iranian military forces 49–50, 79
Iranian military machine 95
Iranian officials 88
Iranian policy 43
Iranian power preponderance 7, 91, 104, 107
Iranian power projection 47, 69
Iranian power superiority 63
Iranian Premier Amir Abbas Hoveyda 54
Iranian pursuit of regional dominance 47
Iranian revolution 42–3, 68, 72, 101
Iranian revolutionary government 43, 87–8, 100
Iranian sphere of influence 30
Iranian Superiority 57–8, 60–1, 66, 73, 75, 80, 91, 93
Iranian support 47, 49, 66, 83
Iranians in Jarbala and Narjaf districts 52
Iran's modernization 81
Iran's occupation 90
Iran's power positioning 54
Iran's superiority 92
Iraq and Saudi Arabia 71
Iraqi ambassador 50
Iraqi ambassador to Iran 89
Iraqi and Iranian military forces 53
Iraqi army 79–80
Iraqi Communist Central Committee 83
Iraqi consolidation 104

Iraqi expulsion of Iranian citizens 90
Iraqi fears 108
Iraqi government 48, 50, 68, 80, 88–9, 98, 105
Iraqi hardware 96
Iraqi insecurity 107
Iraqi interaction 88
Iraqi jets 39, 90
Iraqi leadership 47
Iraqi military development 72
Iraqi military material 61
Iraqi mistreatment of Iranians 49
Iraqi naval plans 71
Iraqi population 47, 88
Iraqi president Ahmed Hassan 50
Iraqi security 43, 47, 87
Iraqi servicemen 64
Iraqi Shi'ites 47, 89
Iraqi submission to Iranian dominance 104
Iraq's authority 51
Iraq's interests 50
Islamic extremists 99–100
Islamic revolution 87–8
issue contention 11, 109
issue interaction 18
issue salience 12, 14–15, 19, 22–3, 44
Issues and Foreign Policy Behavior 12
Italy 78–9

Khomeini 87–8, 96
Kurdish guerrilla movement in Iraq 66
Kurdish movement 50, 83
Kurdish movement in Iraq 49
Kurdish separatist movement 34, 47, 69, 87
Kurdish separatist movement in Iraq 55
Kuwait 53

Literacy Corps 65
London Treaty 7, 42, 47–8, 51, 56, 66

military equipment 37, 39, 78
military expenditure 37–8, 60, 76–80, 94, 96
military forces 48, 69, 90, 98
military modernization 38, 57, 61, 78, 95

## Index

military personnel 37, 60–1, 77, 94–5
military power 4, 37–8, 40, 48, 60, 76, 94
military power capabilities 5, 37–8
military power indicators 77, 95
modernization 61–3, 83–4
Muslim People's Republican Party 97

Najaf 69, 88–9
nation-state creation 20
national power 2, 34, 36–8, 41, 57, 103
nationalism 15
normalization of diplomatic relations 43, 68
Northern Iraq 50, 104

onset of war 30, 33, 41–3, 104
opposition 51–2, 64, 72, 82, 97
opposition groups 81–2
outlying areas 81

Persian Gulf 7, 29, 46–7, 49–50, 54, 69, 71, 89–90
Persian Gulf area 54, 70
petroleum prices 68–9
political identity 87
population 16, 23–4, 38, 64, 81, 87–8; urban 37, 57–8, 74, 92
power 2, 4, 6–7, 10, 30–6, 39, 41, 45, 63, 66, 69, 72–3, 83, 87, 95; pole of 13; realized 36, 38; role of 2, 4, 10, 30, 35, 109
power analysis 6–7, 9, 11, 30, 33–4, 45
power arguments 30–1
power capabilities 7–9, 18–19, 31–2, 34–9, 46, 66, 80–1, 85, 99, 107, 109
power convergence 41–2, 75, 94, 108; rapid 107–8
power conversion factors 36, 57, 95
power distribution 4, 28, 33
power picture 92, 95
power position, comparative 33–4, 45, 56, 65, 96
power preponderance 4, 30–3
power preponderance theory 32–4, 42
power theorists 30–1
power transition theorists 33–4
power transition theory 8–9, 31, 33–6, 39, 41, 44–5, 66, 104, 107–8
protest 51–2, 87

Reciprocal Conflict Spiral 88
reciprocity 6, 25–8, 41, 45, 54, 67, 73, 90; bilateral 28; contingent 52–3
regime 21, 55, 65, 82, 100; imperial 81
regime type 10, 18, 44
regional dominance 22, 42, 46–8, 52, 66, 68–70, 85, 104
relations, cooperative 85, 88
relations post-Algiers 71, 105
relationship, cooperative 27, 85, 105, 107
religious leaders 52, 82, 98
resources, distribution of 31
revolutionary government 7, 86–7, 89–90, 95, 97–9
revolutionary guards 97, 99

Saddam Hussein 5, 51, 56, 70, 98, 100
salience 6, 14–15, 18–19, 22–4, 45
Salient Issues 5, 47–8, 66, 69, 84, 101
Saudi Arabia 50, 54, 71–2
security 8, 13, 23, 48, 51, 54, 69–70, 84, 98, 101, 105–6, 109
security pact 50–1
Shah 7, 43, 46, 48–9, 52–4, 64–5, 69–73, 79, 81–2, 85, 88, 95–100
Shah of Iran 29, 56
skilled workers 99
social stability 38, 57, 63, 65, 80, 84, 95–6, 100
Southern Iraq 51–2
sovereignty 15, 20, 51, 69, 90
Soviet Union 17, 26, 35, 80
stakes 1, 13, 17, 21–2, 46, 48, 56, 106, 109
state behavior 10, 12, 22, 109
state consolidation 42, 46–8
statehood 21
state's ability 37–8
Strait of Hormuz 51–2, 54, 89–90
strategy 25, 27, 36, 46, 52
superiority 56, 58–60, 73–5, 91–4
suppression 82–3
survival 20–1, 23, 43, 48, 86–8, 101
Sympathy 21

tangibility 14–15, 17, 23; dimensions of 23–4
tangible values 22–4, 46–7
Tehran 49, 51–2, 61, 71–3, 81, 89, 95, 99

territory 4, 6, 15–16, 20, 24, 47, 69
threat 4, 21, 47–8, 51–3, 69, 84, 87, 90, 98; direct 7, 43, 47, 51, 105
transition 8, 34–6, 42, 45, 77, 91, 96, 102, 108
troops 30, 37, 50, 53
Turkic Iranians 98
Turkic movement 97

values 12–13, 15–16, 21–3, 33, 67, 106; intangible 23, 47–8, 87
violence, political 2

War: likelihood of 35–6; precipice of 7, 9, 101, 104
war causation 4, 6–8, 11, 20, 30, 32, 35, 40, 103, 108

# ROUTLEDGE INTERNATIONAL HANDBOOKS

*Routledge International Handbooks* is an outstanding, award-winning series that provides cutting-edge overviews of classic research, current research and future trends in Social Science, Humanities and STM.

**Each *Handbook*:**

- is introduced and contextualised by leading figures in the field
- features specially commissioned original essays
- draws upon an international team of expert contributors
- provides a comprehensive overview of a sub-discipline.

*Routledge International Handbooks* aim to address new developments in the sphere, while at the same time providing an authoritative guide to theory and method, the key sub-disciplines and the primary debates of today.

If you would like more information on our on-going *Handbooks* publishing programme, please contact us.

**Tel: +44 (0)20 701 76566**
**Email: reference@routledge.com**

## www.routledge.com/reference

# Routledge Paperbacks Direct

Bringing you the cream of our hardback publishing at paperback prices

This exciting new initiative makes the best of our hardback publishing available in paperback format for authors and individual customers.

Routledge Paperbacks Direct is an ever-evolving programme with new titles being added regularly.

To take a look at the titles available, visit our website.

**www.routledgepaperbacksdirect.com**

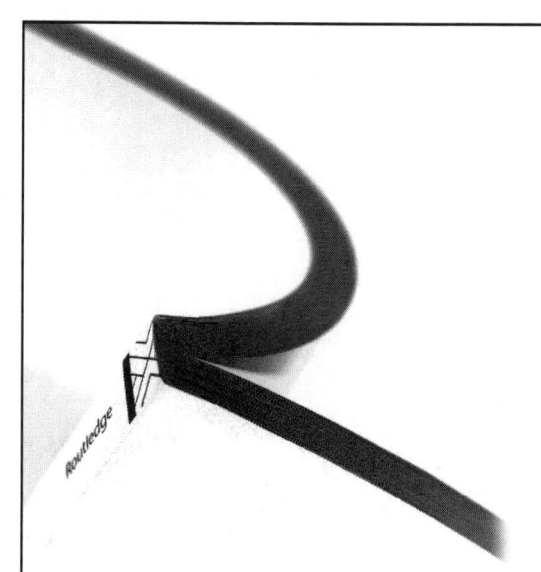

Routledge
Taylor & Francis Group

# ROUTLEDGE Revivals

## Are there some elusive titles you've been searching for but thought you'd never be able to find?

Well this may be the end of your quest. We now offer a fantastic opportunity to discover past brilliance and purchase previously out of print and unavailable titles by some of the greatest academic scholars of the last 120 years.

*Routledge Revivals* is an exciting new programme whereby key titles from the distinguished and extensive backlists of the many acclaimed imprints associated with Routledge are re-issued.

The programme draws upon the backlists of Kegan Paul, Trench & Trubner, Routledge & Kegan Paul, Methuen, Allen & Unwin and Routledge itself.

*Routledge Revivals* spans the whole of the Humanities and Social Sciences, and includes works by scholars such as Emile Durkheim, Max Weber, Simone Weil and Martin Buber.

### FOR MORE INFORMATION

Please email us at **reference@routledge.com** or visit:
**www.routledge.com/books/series/Routledge_Revivals**

www.routledge.com

**Routledge**
Taylor & Francis Group

New eBook Library Collection

**Taylor & Francis eBooks**
Taylor & Francis Group

# eFocus on Globalization

*30 day free trials available!*

This new **multi-disciplinary** collection approaches Globalization from a wide range of perspectives, including:

- Economics
- Business
- History
- Politics
- Geography
- Security
- Sociology
- Education
- Media
- Culture.

Titles included cover the development impact on non western societies as well as on the west. The collection includes contributions which challenge the whole concept of Globalization as well as those that advance it.

Contributions from renowned authorities, the very best in academia...

Key authors include: **Ernesto Zedillo**, Yale University, USA; **Jeffrey Freiden**, Harvard University, USA; **Akbar S. Ahmed**, American University, Washington, USA; **Teressa Brennan**, **V. Spike Peterson**, University of Arizona, USA; **James Mittelman**, Helsinki University, Finland; and **Doug Guthrie**, Stern School of Business, New York University, USA.

The collection includes key works of reference:
- *A Dictionary of Globalization*
- *Globalization; Key Concepts*
- *Globalization*

As well as some **cutting-edge** works such as:
- *The End Game of Globalization* – **Neil Smith**, Graduate Center, City University of New York, USA.
- *A Globalizing World?* – **David Held**, London School of Economics, UK.

eFocus on Globalization is available as a subscription package of 80 titles with 10 new eBooks per annum.

*Recommend this package to your librarian today!*

Order now for guaranteed capped price increase.

For a complete list of titles, visit:
**www.ebooksubscriptions.com/eFocusGlobalization**
www.ebooksubscriptions.com

---

For more information, pricing enquiries or to order a free trial, please contact your local online sales team:

**UK and Rest of the world**
Tel: +44 (0) 20 7017 6062
Email: online.sales@tandf.co.uk

**United States, Canada and South America**
Tel: 1-888-318-2367
Email: e-reference@taylorandfrancis.com